The Examined Life Workbook:

A bold journey toward knowing yourself

Brittany Salsman

Brittany Salsman, Life Lived by Design
Chicago, IL
The Examined Life Workbook
Self-published
brittany@lifelivedbydesign.com
www.lifelivedbydesign.com

Author photo by Lens to Heart Photography
Cover design by Carleen Sinton

For additional copies or bulk purchases of this book, please contact t us at the email above.

American
Brain Tumor
Association®

Providing and pursuing answers®

Table of Contents

Part Three: There

In Dedication To:

Christin Salsman
Simply put, you are my rock.

Part One:
Before

Everyone wants to be known. That begins with knowing yourself.

It was January 2, 2017 - a Monday. I was having lunch with a friend and noticed the first signs of a developing migraine. It started in my right temple with a low, constant tension. As lunch progressed, the tension grew into an ache and shifted to just above my right ear.

I didn't think much of it because I've had many migraines before. They make an appearance about 3-4 times each year, so I knew it would continue to increase in pain as it shifted around to the base of my neck before disappearing. I also knew exactly what was needed to manage it until it went away. Go home, take two migraine-strength Tylenol tablets, turn off the lights, climb under the blankets, and sleep for about two hours. This is precisely what I did and when I woke up, I felt great!

Then, about an hour later, the migraine came back with a vengeance. This had not happened before, which was interesting, but not alarming. I simply took a couple more capsules and went back to sleep for the night.

The next morning, I had slept off my migraine and prepared to go back to work after the holiday break. It was an average workday - not too busy, not too slow. But the one thing that wasn't average was the lightning bolts that would dart through my right eye. They were quick, infrequent, and didn't impact my ability to do my work, but I noticed them.

By Wednesday, those short bursts of light shifted to complete blackouts in my right eye for 5-10 seconds at a time. While this worried me, I decided to give it until the weekend to improve before I called a doctor. My coworker, on the other hand, was very concerned. She's a very level-headed person, so when she urged me to go to an immediate care center after work, I paid attention.

When I arrived at the immediate care center, thankfully, no one was ahead of me and I went right back. I expected they would prescribe an even stronger migraine medication than I had at home and send me on my way. Instead, they administered a vision test and told me I needed to go to the hospital. They offered to call an ambulance, but I still didn't think it was that serious. So, I walked the six blocks to Northwestern Memorial Hospital.

After five hours in the waiting room, I was exhausted and happy to hear my name called. The ER doctor ordered a CT scan and came back shortly to say, "The CT shows that there's a mass, but it's probably not a big deal. We will need to admit you and run more tests, so I'm going to have the nurse give you some medication to manage the pain you're in." The nurse then injected my IV with pain meds and off to la-la land I went.

From that point on, my memory is blank with the exception of two moments. One of my younger sisters playing the ukulele and singing and a second of my older sister and my dad walking behind me as I was transported to the surgical prep room. I don't remember anything outside of that. Now, I know what happened because people have told me, but I don't have any personal memory. No memory of being officially admitted from the ER and moving to a hospital room. No memory of the MRI. No memory of receiving the diagnosis. No memory of my family arriving. No memories of interactions with my medical team. No memories of the discussion around my medical options or the subsequent surgery to remove a 2.6 cm meningioma, a type of brain tumor, that Friday, January 6, 2017. No memory of my time in the ICU, being moved out of the ICU, or being discharged. No memory of the ride home, walking in my door, or seeing my dog, Taz, for the first time. No memory of sleeping in my bed that first night back at home. There's a large gap of time that is simply blank in my mind.

 To see photos from my surgery and recovery, scan the QR code here or visit www.lifelivedbydesign.com/surgery.

This experience was life-altering and marked the beginning of the examination of my own life. My life - the way I make decisions, interact with others, prioritize what is most important, and the clarity I have around what I'm moving towards - is completely different after January 6, 2017. There is a clear distinction between the way I moved through the world before my surgery and the way I move through life now. I seek approval only from myself. I know I have the answers to all my questions within me. I am deeply tapped into what I truly want, rather than what others want for me. I experience the richness of life every single day.

As I have connected with others who have had life-altering experiences, I have found that this is not uncommon. In fact, psychologists Richard Tedeschi and Lawrence Calhoun coined the term "posttraumatic growth" in the mid-1990s to describe just this. "Posttraumatic growth is the experience of positive change that occurs as a result of the struggle with highly challenging life crises. It is manifested in a variety of ways, including an increased appreciation for life in general, more meaningful interpersonal relationships, an increased sense of personal strength, changed priorities, and a richer existential and spiritual life."[1]

When you look your own mortality directly in the eyes, it is simply impossible to ignore. You are left with a single decision - continue on the path of overwhelm, disappointment, and dissatisfaction that you're on or pick yourself up and do something about it.

I am grateful for my brain tumor and, in an even stranger way, I am also grateful that my medical team was not able to remove all of it. I return to Northwestern Memorial Hospital annually for MRI scans to monitor the residual tumor. This provides me with the opportunity to assess the progress I've made on my personal commitment to "love the life [I] live and live the life [I] love."

This is the moment my "why" was born and this workbook is a manifestation of the bold journey I have been on since my surgery. My desire is to share tools and strategies that will help you design your life more intentionally - to help you move from "why me" to "because me." I'm offering you the opportunity to know yourself first on an extremely intimate level. I'm calling this "non-traumatic growth." I want every single person to experience the awakening that I had without having to experience a life-altering event such as mine. For you to move toward a place where there is nothing in your life that prompts you to say, "I don't know why that's there." Everything in your life, everyone in your life, every action you take, every decision you make serves the purpose of taking you one step closer to your true self.

---

[1]Tedeschi, Richard G. & Calhoun, Lawrence G. (2004). Posttraumatic Growth: Conceptual Foundations and Empirical Evidence. *Psychological Inquiry, 15*(1), 1-18. https://www.tandfonline.com/doi/abs/10.1207/s15327965pli1501_01

For those of you who chose this workbook because you feel stuck or apathetic about your life, this journey will challenge you to stop living passively and take control of your life again. You are the CEO of your life and it's time to formally step into this role.

For those of you who chose this workbook because you are overwhelmed by the pressure of accomplishment and the weight of others' needs and desires, this journey will challenge you to take a breather and learn how to trust yourself first. You have to stop taking action for a brief moment so you can take inventory of all things 'you.'

This workbook is divided into four parts - Before, Here, There, and Between. 'Part One: Before' lays the foundation for success in completing this workbook. It includes setting your intentions and developing a plan. 'Part Two: Here' provides an opportunity to fully audit all aspects your life as it currently exists. This is not intended to be an opportunity to self-judge or immediately change things. Instead, it's an opportunity to notice the way you currently move through the world and learn about who you are now. From this perspective, you'll launch into 'Part Three: There' which is future-oriented. This is the section where you'll imagine possibilities, dream big, and discover what's holding you back. Just as with part two, I encourage you to release any urges to take action or start making changes during part three as well. 'Part Four: Between' is where the rubber hits the road so-to-speak. You will compile your action ideas from the previous sections, prioritize them, and develop a plan to make your future vision a reality.

As you progress through each part, don't worry about whether your reflections, thoughts, and responses are right or wrong, good or bad. There are no right or wrong answers, nor is there a good or bad approach to this workbook. Instead, consider what is useful and what is not useful. Not every exercise and activity will be useful for every person. Be curious about yourself. Find the lessons that resonate with you and release the ones that don't. The key is how you make it useful to you. When you catch yourself asking, "What does she mean by this?" or "What is this question asking?" instead ask yourself, "What meaning do I make from this?" or "What do I need this question to ask?"

I recommend that you take your time with this workbook. Allow this workbook to serve as a guide as you explore all aspects of your life, get to know yourself more thoroughly, gain clarity around your future, and step into the person you want to become. For me, this happened over the course of several long road trips - anywhere from one week to two months on the road at a time - and continues to evolve today. For you, it might also be a long road trip, or a weekend getaway, or simply locking yourself in a room for a few hours each week. Where you do it is not as important as how you do it.

Here are some foundational suggestions that will help you get the most out of this workbook:

- **Disconnect.** In order to truly know yourself, all outside influences need to be removed from the equation. Turn off your phone. Not silence, but actually power it down. Let those in your life know that you'll be unavailable so they don't worry and can support you through this process.

- **Growth mindset.** You will quickly learn in this process that becoming the person you want to become is deeply rooted in your own mindset, not dependent on factors external to yourself. Lean into developing the belief that you are the expert on yourself, that you are 100% resourceful, that you will learn what is needed as you go, and that these together allow you to bring that future version of yourself into reality. If you find that your responses are getting redundant, this may indicate that you're not being completely honest with yourself or that you have already done some work toward knowing yourself. In these moments, remind yourself to lean into a growth mindset to learn more about the possibilities of what could be.

- **Pace yourself.** There is no reward for finishing this workbook in a single sitting. The reward is in the growth you will experience over time. If you feel yourself getting overwhelmed, take a break. If you find that you're not experiencing new insights, take a break. Both of these are indicators that your brain has reached capacity.

- **Journal.** You may find it useful to utilize a journal or notebook alongside this workbook in the cases where you need more space or would rather draw than write. Don't let the space provided in this workbook limit your reflection, imagination, creativity, and insight generation. Use the margins, highlight, underline, and circle. Make it your own.

- **Ask why.** As you progress through each activity and the reflection prompts, continue to dig deeper. If a thought or answer comes quickly or easily, ask yourself why. If you are stumped or are drawing a blank, ask yourself why. While there are hundreds of reflection questions throughout this process, the most powerful one of all is a single word - why?

- **Resist action.** At least until part four: Between. It's not that I don't want you to take action at all, but the lasting impact of this journey derives from increasing your self-awareness. This is tougher to do if you're always taking action and not giving yourself space to simply sit with what is present. Use the "ideas for action" space at the end of each activity in parts two and three or the "notes" pages in the back of this workbook to keep a running record of the action you want to take. This way they are not forgotten. Then, when it comes time to take action in part four, you can make strategic choices based on your overall learning and growth rather than on impulse or nature.

- **Come back.** After you've completed the full workbook, choose a time to come back as a way to check in on your progress and intentionally adjust your trajectory. Some activities that don't resonate now will at a later time and vice versa. It might be tempting to choose the start of a new year to go through this process. I encourage you to find a time that is significant for you. For me, I come back to this process each August, which aligns with my regular MRI checkups. It's a way to ground myself in all the reasons why I started this journey. What time of year can serve as that anchor for you?

- **Seek assistance.** It is important to note that this workbook is not a replacement for working directly with a life coach or a therapist. Listen to your needs and ask for support when and where you need it.

You are about to embark on a bold journey toward knowing yourself - learning who you are, what you dream of, and how it manifests into reality. You will look past your demographics and identify your psychographics - your attitudes, interests, opinions, beliefs, and actions. This is intentionally not your traditional self-help book. I'm not here to tell you the ten steps to awakening, the seven habits of successful people, or the three character traits of leaders. It is impossible for me to know what you need to do because I am not you. You have the answers within you. This journey creates the space (both literally and figuratively) to dust out the corners and shine a light on aspects of your being you might not have known were there.

Most importantly, to get the most out of this workbook and journey, you have to do the work. Don't simply read through the activities and think about them in your mind. Don't look forward in the workbook with the plan to return to a particular activity when you have more time. This workbook is sequenced with intention and care. It's time to show up for yourself. Today, commit to yourself that you will take on this bold journey in the order laid out here and by the directions provided. Once you've gone through the entire workbook the first time, feel free to come back to the activities you most need, especially as you experience new and changing 'seasons' in life. Be open to the possibilities. No matter how crazy an activity might sound, do it anyway.

You'll also find a couple of icons throughout the workbook. These are key moments for additional resources or support.

 While working with a coach through any individual activity or through the workbook as a whole is highly recommended, this icon indicates that a coach could provide even deeper insights for that particular activity. If you choose to work with Life Lived by Design, mention this workbook for a 5% discount on a coaching package.

 Throughout the workbook, you'll find QR codes which indicate there are digital resources available online to aid in doing this work. Simply scan the code or visit the website listed for each activity.

Lastly, to help others experience the lasting impact of non-traumatic growth, I would be incredibly grateful if you would generously offer a five-star review of this workbook once you're finished.

Create Your Plan

Today's Date: _____

When you consider potential obstacles, create a plan for yourself, and determine how you will celebrate successes before you even begin, you are more likely to follow through on your intentions. With this in mind, create a plan for completing this workbook. Take a moment to consider these questions:

How frequently and for how long in each sitting will I carve out to do this work? (e.g., once a week for two hours, every day for 30 minutes, every third Wednesday for half a day)

Where will I go to do this work? (e.g., in my room, my office, to the park, the library, a place of worship)

What do I need with me while I do this work? (e.g., a glass of water, quiet music, a journal, comfortable clothes)

Who do I want or need to tell about my plan? (e.g., a best friend, my spouse, a sibling, a mentor)

If I have family or roommates living with me, what do I need from them to be successful in following through?

How will I hold myself accountable to my plan? (e.g., marking my calendar, rewards, accountability buddy, shutting off my phone)

How will I celebrate completing Part 2: Here? (e.g., take a three-day break from the workbook, enjoy a movie night)

How will I celebrate completing Part 3: There? (e.g., take an afternoon drive for fresh air, have a family game night)

How will I celebrate completing the entire workbook? (e.g., a special dinner, a dance party, a new outfit, a day doing only what I most want)

Set Your Intentions

Today's Date: _____

While you may or may not have a clear idea of what life holds in store for you five, ten, or twenty years from now, it is important to take a moment to set your intentions for the time you intend to spend on this workbook. This activity will not only help you clarify your intentions, but when complete, will also serve as a motivational tool when you need a nudge to return to the workbook.

The date by which I intent to complete this workbook is _____.

Who do I want to become by the date listed above?

Imagine that I'm waking up on the above date as the person I just described. What would be true?

How do I spend the day?

What do I love about this day?

Backing up to the week before this day, what specifically do I need to do in order to wake up on the date above as I just described?

Backing up to the month before this day, what specifically do I need to do in order to wake up on the date above as I just described?

What do I need to start doing right now to take the first step on this path?

What do I need to stop doing right now to step toward this intention?

What character traits do I hope to strengthen along the journey?

What do I hope to learn about myself along the journey?

What do I hope this process will teach me?

Now, fast forward to the date I listed above and imagine that all of this has come true. What am I most proud of?

Take a moment to read through your responses from beginning to end. As you read them, what song comes to mind as an anthem for this story?

The above responses serve as the foundation of a vision recording that you can leverage as a motivator throughout this process. This recording can be a video or simply an audio recording on your phone. Leverage the medium you feel will be most useful to you.

1. Fill in any gaps in your script above. What else will be true on the date you listed above? What message do you most want to include?

2. Revisit your script and adjust the tense so it reads as if everything has already been accomplished. For example, instead of, "I will complete all activities in *The Examined Life Workbook*," say, "I have completed all activities in *The Examined Life Workbook*."

3. Record yourself reading the script with the confidence of everything having come to reality.

4. Include a song in the background to add extra meaning and emotion.

5. Decide how you will leverage your recording. You can play it each time you sit down to work on your workbook, each time you complete an activity, each time you have an ah-ha moment, each morning, each evening. The uses are endless. When will you most need a boost in this process?

Scan the QR code here or visit www.lifelivedbydesign.com/intentions to hear a few vision recordings I've crafted on my journey.

Wheel of Emotions

Today's Date: _____

You are an emotional being. Even if you do not outwardly express emotions easily, you still experience them. In fact, your emotions are the place from which you take action. You respond differently from a place of anger than excitement. The circumstances of the situation could be identical, but it's the feeling that influences your actions most.

As you begin this work, center yourself and identify the emotion or emotions you are experiencing in this moment.

1. Start at the center of the wheel on the next page to identify the initial feeling.
2. Move to the middle ring of emotions from that place to be even more specific.
3. Shift to the outer most ring and choose the feeling that most resonates.
4. Repeat these steps until all emotions have been identified.

For example, you may be happy to do this work and also fearful of what might come up. When you dig into feeling happy in the second ring, you might identify it more specifically as interested and further as curious in the third ring. You might also identify happiness as optimistic in the second ring and further as inspired in the third ring. On the other side, as you further acknowledge the fear, you might learn that it's anxiousness and further worrying when you get to the outer most ring. Therefore, the three core emotions would be curious, inspired, and worrying.

From this place of identification, you can then explore these emotions from a position of learning and growth.

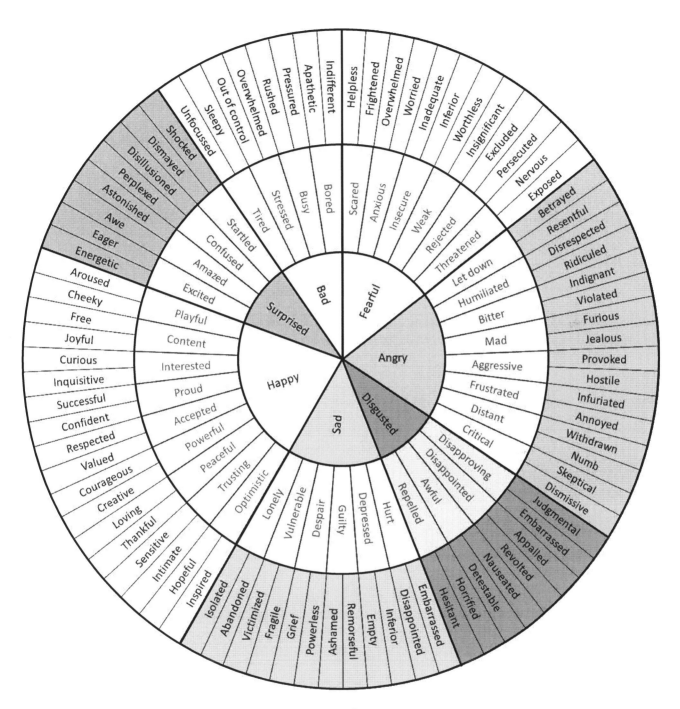

These are the specific emotions I am experiencing right now:

_____ _____ _____

Take a moment to consider these questions:

What is the message behind each of these emotions?

What are each of these emotions trying to teach me?

How are each of these emotions useful?

What do I notice when I allow each of these emotions to be present?

How do I want to move forward with each of these emotions?

What do I want to let go of?

TIP: This workbook is meant to serve as a foundation for examining all aspects of your life. Because of this, you will likely experience a range of emotions along the journey. Rather than avoiding, rejecting, or ignoring these emotions, acknowledge and embrace them as opportunities for additional learning. At any point, and especially when you experience an emotion you cannot identify, come back to this activity to check in with your feelings and seek deeper learning.

Part Two: Here

Love the life you live.

-Bob Marley

Brain Dump

Today's Date: _____

Before you begin discovering where you are now in your life, let's take a moment to clear your brain of clutter. Pull out a timer and set it for five minutes. Press start and use this space to free write for the entire time. Don't worry about spelling, grammar, incomplete sentences, or legibility. Simply write whatever comes to mind in whatever order it comes. You may even decide to draw instead of writing words or a combination of art and words. Whatever you choose, let the pen flow, and don't stop until the timer sounds.

No one will be reading this except you and those with whom you choose to share it, so let your thoughts flow freely. The purpose of this activity is to declutter your mind so you can be fully present with the activities. You'll do this at the beginning and end of each part of this workbook.

Ready. Set. Go!

TIP: At moments when you feel your brain is full of competing or varying thoughts, pull out a piece of paper and write down all the thoughts you are having. Be specific enough that you are writing word for word what is going through your mind. Next, categorize each thought as useful, not useful, or neutral. Consider how you can replace less useful thoughts with either neutral or more useful ones. This allows you to take more control over the results you are getting.

Wheel of Life

Today's Date: _____

The Wheel of Life is a meaningful starting point because it provides a great snapshot of where you are currently in different aspects of your life.

1. Start by adjusting any of the categories you see around the circle. Maybe you want to remove, rename, or add new categories. Maybe you want to split a category into subcategories. Go ahead and make the wheel your own. You might also find that the wheel, as it currently exists, suits you well. It's also okay to leave the categories as they are.

2. Consider your level of satisfaction in each wedge independently and give it a score of 1-10, where 1 is "I'm really not satisfied with this area of my life" and 10 is "I'm super satisfied with this area of my life." It's important to consider your current level of satisfaction today, not where you'd like it to be. Write your rating next to each category on your wheel.

3. For the last step, go ahead and shade in each wedge of the wheel to represent the corresponding number. This provides more visual clarity of your snapshot.

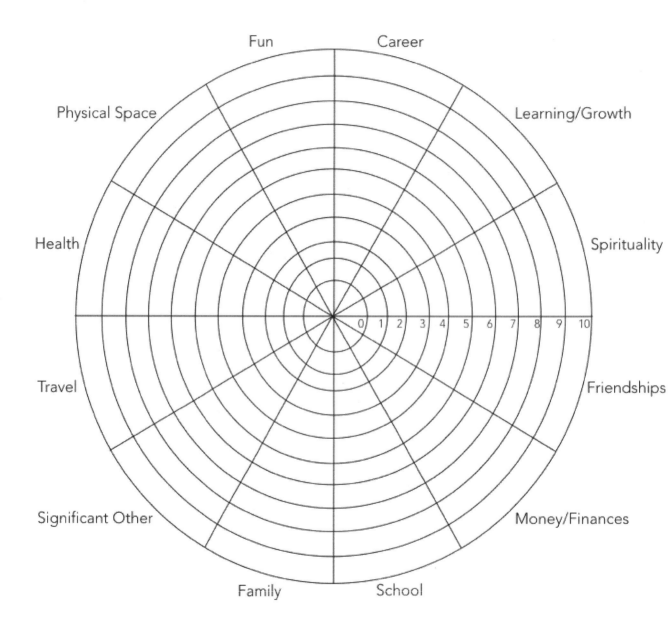

Take a moment to consider these questions:

Other than the numbers themselves, what jumps out at me about my wheel? Why does that jump out at me right now?

What surprises me about my wheel? Why does that surprise me?

What do I notice about connections between different wedges in my wheel?

What do I notice about how bumpy or smooth my wheel is?

Who am I when I'm satisfied?

Who am I when I'm not as satisfied?

What am I learning about myself through this activity?

Ideas for action:

Pouring In Versus Pouring Out

Today's Date: _____

Every day, every hour, every minute, and every second, you are either pouring into yourself or pouring out to others. This activity is designed to assess where you are currently in terms of giving and receiving. Feel free to add or subtract arrows as needed. The purpose of this activity is simply to increase your awareness of how you are pouring into yourself and pouring out to others.

Next to the arrows pointing away from the body, list all the things you do that pour out to others. Pouring out can come in many forms from pouring money, time, energy, and emotion.

Conversely, write all the ways you pour into yourself next to the arrows pointing toward the body. These are the things that revitalize and refresh you. While self-care is certainly part of pouring into yourself, it is much bigger. It includes all of the things that give you energy. Consider how you pour into yourself with money, time, and emotion that results in increased energy.

You might also notice that there is overlap in some areas. Some things that you pour out may also energize you. That's okay! Make a note of that too.

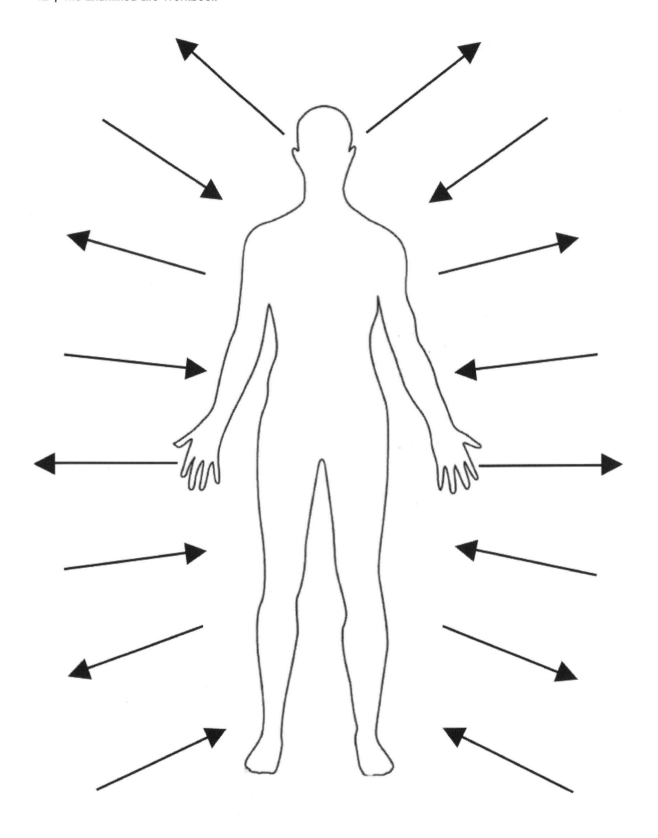

Take a moment to consider these questions:

What do I notice about how I'm giving and receiving energy? Why does that stand out?

What's my current relationship with balancing what I pour out to others and what I pour into myself?

What am I tolerating in my life? Why?

What is irritating me? Why?

Where am I letting negativity creep in? Why?

How do "needs" or "necessity" show up in my chart?

How do "wants" or "desires" show up in my chart?

What things on my chart do I need to let go of? Why?

What am I exhilarated by? Why?

What am I eager to receive or give? Why?

What things on my chart do I need to increase? Why?

Where do I need to tighten my boundaries? Why?

What specifically has contributed to my current balance in giving and receiving?

Who am I trying to please? Why?

What am I learning about myself through this activity?

Ideas for action:

Your Inner Child

Today's Date: _____

Before you were inundated with messages from the media, impressions from friends, influence of societal expectations, and pressure from family, you had a belief about the life you would live. I'll bet it did not include working ridiculously long hours, always being aware of what you eat, living paycheck to paycheck, and talking down to yourself.

Nope! Your younger self played endlessly while tapping into your imagination. You ate what you wanted when you wanted without shame, made it clear when it was time to take a nap, and dreamed wildly about the amazingly fulfilled life you would have when you grew up.

Something happened between then and now. When someone gave you a box at the age of five, you turned it into something that took you to entirely new places. Now when someone gives you a box, you try to fit within its parameters. The imagination, creativity, and dream is diminished at best and completely gone at worst. You doubt yourself. You question your ability to bring your dreams to reality. You adjust and accommodate to keep others happy. You put yourself on the back burner. You step inside the box and conform.

Today, your younger self has a message for you. To hear what your 5-year-old self has to say, scan the QR code here or visit www.lifelivedbydesign.com/inner-child. Before pressing play, find a comfortable space - one where you will not be interrupted. Allow your imagination to lead the way. As you listen, try not to be so worried about seeing a clear scene. That's not what is important. What is important is the learning that comes from this activity.

Notes:

After hearing the message from your younger self, take a moment to consider these questions:

What advice did my inner child have for me today?

What was surprising to hear from my inner child? Why was that surprising?

What was the most challenging thing to hear from my inner child? Why?

What does my inner child want me to do more of? Why?

What does my inner child want me to do less of? Why?

What was the core message my inner child had for me?

What do I want my inner child to know?

What would I be able to accomplish if I never broke another promise I made to myself?

What am I learning about myself through this activity?

Ideas for action:

TIP: This might be a great moment to revisit the Wheel of Emotions on page 26.

<u>Values Exemplified</u>

Today's Date: _____

Getting clear on what I value in life was a critical first step in this journey for me. Gaining clarity on my values uncovered aspects of what motivates me and things I might want to avoid in life. From this foundation, I began making more informed decisions for myself and took active steps toward designing a life that aligns with and exemplifies these values.

As I have gotten to know myself better and as priorities have shifted, so have my values. While values are a cornerstone of who you are, they are not unchangeable.

1. On the next two pages, mark through any word that does not resonate with you as something you value. If you value something that is not on the list, go ahead and write it in on the extra lines.

Accountability	Community	Education	Fulfillment
Achievement	Companionship	Effectiveness	Fun
Adaptability	Compassion	Efficiency	Generosity
Advancement	Competence	Environment	Grace
Adventure	Competition	Ethical practice	Gratitude
Affection	Confidence	Equality	Growth
Altruism	Conformity	Equity	Happiness
Authenticity	Connection	Ethics	Harmony
Authority	Contentment	Excellence	Health
Autonomy	Contribution	Excitement	Home
Balance	Cooperation	Expertise	Honesty
Beauty	Courage	Fairness	Humility
Belonging	Creativity	Faith	Humor
Boldness	Curiosity	Fame	Impact
Challenge	Decisiveness	Family	Inclusion
Change	Determination	Foregiveness	Independence
Collaboration	Dignity	Freedom	Influence
Commitment	Diversity	Friendship	Initiative

Integrity	Patience	Safety	Truth
Intelligence	Patriotism	Security	Uniqueness
Intimacy	Peace	Serenity	Variety
Involvement	Perseverance	Service	Vulnerability
Justice	Pleasure	Simplicity	Wealth
Kindness	Power	Sophistication	Whole-heartedness
Knowledge	Privacy	Spirituality	Wisdom
Leadership	Purity	Spontaneity	Work
Learning	Quality	Stability	_____
Leisure	Quantity	Status	_____
Love	Recognition	Stewardship	_____
Loyalty	Reliability	Success	_____
Merit	Religion	Teamwork	_____
Money	Reputation	Time	_____
Nature	Resourceful	Tradition	_____
Openness	Respect	Tranquility	_____
Optimism	Responsibility	Travel	_____
Order	Risk-Taking	Trust	

2. Next, of the remaining words, circle 10-15 that you highly value.

3. Now, of the 10-15 that you circled, place a star next to the five words that spark something within you.

4. Finally, of the five words you placed a star next to, list here the three that you absolutely cannot live without.

_____   _____   _____

Take a moment to consider these questions:

What surprised me during this process? Why was this surprising?

How does each of these values show up in various aspects of my life? Feel free to look back at the Wheel of Life on page 35 for assistance.

What impact does each of these values have on my daily decisions and activities?

How can I more fully express each of these values in my daily actions?

How does holding each of these values influence others' perceptions of me (both good and not so good)?

What would happen in one year if I were to make every single decision based on these values?

What am I learning about myself through this activity?

Ideas for action:

Your Truth

Today's Date: _____

Along with the values you identified in the previous activity, your personal truths greatly influence how you show up every day. Early in life, you received cues from community leaders, society, and most impactfully, your family about what is true and why it is true. However, at some point in your journey, opportunities began to present themselves that challenged or questioned those truths, which either shifted or reaffirmed them. This process occurs so gradually that you likely transitioned into adulthood having rarely examined your collection of truths. This activity allows space for just that.

Take a moment to consider these questions:

How do I define truth?

What are my truths about religion, faith, or spirituality? How do I know these to be true?

What are my truths about politics? How do I know these to be true?

What are my truths about human nature? How do I know these to be true?

What are my truths about money? How do I know these to be true?

What are my truths about education? How do I know these to be true?

What are my truths about work? How do I know these to be true?

What are my truths about family? How do I know these to be true?

What are my truths about gender and gender roles? How do I know these to be true?

What are my truths about race? How do I know these to be true?

What are my truths about sexual orientation? How do I know these to be true?

What are my truths about myself? How do I know these to be true?

How have my truths evolved?

Who or what influences my truths? Why?

When was a moment that my truths were tested or challenged?

What did that test or challenge teach me?

How do my collective truths shape my daily actions?

How do my collective truths shape my relationships?

What truths are no longer serving me that I need to let go of? Why?

What truths do I need to double down on? Why?

Which of my truths are in contradiction with one another?

What would happen if I fully lived out all of my truths?

What am I learning about myself through this activity?

Ideas for action:

TIP: This might be a great moment to revisit the Wheel of Emotions on page 26.

Training Elephants

Today's Date: _____

Elephants begin their training as a baby. A rope is tied around their foot and the other end is tied to a stake in the ground. Consequently, they stay within the radius of the rope. They could easily pull the stake from the ground or their foot out of the rope, but they don't. This rope, and the lack of fighting from the baby elephant, allows the trainers to work with them and teach them with very minimal effort.

Then, as the baby elephant grows into an adult elephant, the rope is removed from its foot, and the stake is no longer needed. They still do not go anywhere, though. They stay within that radius in which they've been trained.

What are all the ways that you condition yourself to live in a bubble? Better yet, what are all the ways you allow other people to condition you to live within a bubble? You allow other people to define how you should live, what you should do, what your accomplishments should be, what your family should look like, and what your career should entail. Instead, you should pull that stake out of the ground and listen to your own inner heart - your inner voice - and do what your heart desires. You should not pay attention to what others have conditioned you to think or believe.

Take a moment to consider these questions:

What is the rope that's holding me back? Why?

What does my stake represent? Why?

Who has control over the thing my rope is tethered to? Why?

What could I accomplish without the rope?

How am I getting in my own way?

How am I lifting myself up?

How am I breaking free?

What am I learning about myself through this activity?

Ideas for action:

Love List

Today's Date: _____

I often hear the phrase "checking all the boxes" when I'm working with clients who feel stuck or dissatisfied. It usually comes with the sentiment of doing all "the right" things, but not finding happiness. You also have a checklist for your life - the things you want or need to accomplish. Your checklist includes aspects of your career, family, health, friendships, finances, the home you create, and for some, your spirituality. There are many things that get put next to a box on this list that you then strive to check off.

Your level of satisfaction with life comes down to who is putting the items on your list. Is the list being created by you or someone else? Does the list come from societal expectations, from parents, from friends, from a spouse, or does it come from you? Does it come from something external or do you fully own and truly desire to accomplish every single thing on that list?

I've found that clients who come to me stuck or dissatisfied typically have a list that's at least partially created by someone or something else (e.g., family, supervisor, societal expectations, the media). They're doing all the things they think others expect of them, but they haven't been honest with themselves about whether or not those are the things they actually want.

It's time to get real about your list. First, create a list below that represents all the boxes you have either already checked or are trying to check. Do your best not to judge any item on the list or where it comes from. If you feel any tug or pull toward accomplishing something in your life, add it to your list. As you create this list, consider all aspects of your life. Revisit the categories from the Wheel of Life, if that is helpful.

Create your list here:

- [ ] _____

- [ ] _____

- [ ] _____

- [ ] _____

- [ ] _____

- [ ] _____

- [ ] _____

- [ ] _____

- [ ] _____

- [ ] _____

- [ ] _____

- [ ] _____

- [ ] _____

☐ _____

☐ _____

☐ _____

☐ _____

☐ _____

☐ _____

☐ _____

☐ _____

☐ _____

☐ _____

☐ _____

☐ _____

Now, go back through each item on this list and ask yourself why it made the list. Is it on your list because you truly want it to be there, or has it made the list because of some external expectation or pressure? You may even indicate with + symbol those items you want on your list and with a * symbol those items that comes from external sources.

Take a moment to consider these questions:

Which item(s) was I hesitant to write down? Why?

Which item(s) did I leave off the list even though they should be here? Why were they left off?

Which items need to be removed from my list?

What was my internal dialogue as I completed this list?

What's most present for me as I review the entire list written in front of me?

How true is my list?

What am I learning about myself so far through this activity?

Once you've created your list and reflected upon each item, create a second list. This is a list of all the things you love - from big loves like traveling to new places to small loves like cuddling with a puppy. Consider objects, people, activities, feelings, and experiences. Again, resist the urge to judge what does or doesn't make the list. Simply make it here:

☐ _____   ☐ _____

☐ _____   ☐ _____

☐ _____   ☐ _____

☐ _____   ☐ _____

☐ _____   ☐ _____

☐ _____   ☐ _____

☐ _____   ☐ _____

☐ _____   ☐ _____

☐ _____   ☐ _____

☐ _____   ☐ _____

☐ _____   ☐ _____

Take a moment to consider these questions:

Which item(s) was I hesitant to write down? Why?

Which items did I leave off the list even though they should be here? Why were they left off?

When was the last time I activated each item on my love list?

What was my internal dialogue as I completed this list?

What do I notice about my two lists? Why does that stand out?

To what degree are my two lists integrated? Why or why not?

Ideas for action:

Compass Versus GPS

Today's Date: _____

Are you using a compass or a GPS to guide you through life? There's a big difference between these two. To help you determine which one you're holding, consider the following statements and determine which in each pair most resonates with you.

When I consider an intention…

____ I am able to see multiple paths to accomplishing that intention.

____ I can see exactly what I need to do to bring it to reality.

When I come upon obstacles…

____ I feel challenged and take a moment to consider all of my options.

____ I feel overwhelmed and take a moment for a break.

When I listen to my internal dialogue…

____ I am flexible in considering the best way forward.

____ I am determined to make things work, no matter what.

When I receive feedback…

____ I consider the information to make better decisions.

____ I am confused about how to apply it to my current circumstances.

Flip to page 327 to determine your results. As you review your results, resist the urge to celebrate or knock yourself down. Simply notice what there is to learn.

I am holding a _____ in my hand.

A GPS provides a highlighted route and step-by-step directions to arrive at a predetermined destination. You enter a destination, and it knows where you are currently, so it's going to highlight a route to get you directly from one point to another. Two people who have the same beginning and ending location will take the exact same path.

A compass, on the other hand, provides guidance via true north. The starting location is set, but the destination is optional, and the journey is yet to be determined. Two people who start in the same place could easily end up in two different locations because of their openness to an unlikely journey. This openness is what determines the destination or the outcome. Also, the true north for each person can be different which, of course, ends up in a different outcome.

Someone who's using GPS to guide their decisions typically finds themselves going through the motions of life. When someone who's using GPS comes to an obstacle along the journey, they find themselves looking elsewhere for the answer. They want someone else to solve their problem, and they often blame someone else when things don't go the way they want them to.

On the other hand, someone who uses a compass as their guiding tool, combined with a true north, generally leads a very intentional life in all aspects. When they encounter an obstacle while using a compass, they find themselves asking questions like:

- Which of these options aligns with my true north?
- Which of these options will get me closer to my true north?
- Is there a better option that I'm not even considering?

Determining Your True North

Today's Date: _____

Utilizing a compass alone isn't enough. You need a true north as well. It's the thing you want in life more than anything else. It's the one thing that, if you lost everything else, you'd be okay because you've still got this one thing. For some, that might be money, or recognition, or family, or security. There are all kinds of true norths, and there is no right or wrong answer. Everyone's true north will be different, and it takes time, reflection, and a lot of self-awareness to gain clarity on what your true north is.

Even if someone else has the same true north as you, the outcome will still be different because the conceptualization of it is different. For example, my true north is happiness. I am certain that I am not the only person on this planet with happiness as their true north. However, the outcomes will be different because we each conceptualize happiness in different ways. What makes me happy is not the same thing that makes the next person happy. This results in lives lived in very different ways. Neither right nor wrong, just different.

Let's dig into the beginnings of finding your true north. This is just the beginning because it is not an overnight or one activity discovery. It takes a lot of reflection, self-awareness, honest conversations, and what I like to call personal bluntness. In other words, you have to stop lying to yourself and maybe even call yourself out on your own contradictions. You might find it helpful to refer back to the Values Exemplified activity on page 49 as a starting place. Let's jump in.

1. The one thing that is the most important to me, the one thing that I absolutely cannot live without, the one thing that, if I lost everything else, I'd be okay because I have this one thing left is…

_____

2. What does this one thing bring into my life?

_____

_____

_____

3. What does my response to #2 bring into my life?

_____

_____

_____

4. What does my response to #3 bring into my life?

_____

_____

_____

You might be finding it more challenging to answer this same question the more times it is asked, but that's a good thing. That means you're getting closer to your true north. It means you are digging deep and starting to get honest with yourself. However, you still have a little more work to do to identify it. To do this, keep asking yourself, "What does my previous response bring into my life?" over and over until you get to a place of something so large that it impacts ALL aspects of your life.

If your true north is connected to another person, it is not your true north. A person is not your true north. Not only do people come and go for any number of reasons, but your true north is something that guides every single decision you make. No one other than you should be influencing your decisions. For this reason alone, your true north has to come from within, not from somewhere else.

Use this space to continue to flesh out your true north.

Ideas for action:

Checking Your True North

Today's Date: _____

Once you feel you've identified your true north, check to see if you've peeled back all the layers or if you're still sitting on the surface. You'll circle back in Part Four: Between to explore how you can leverage your true north. For now, just test it out to see if there's more digging that needs to be done. Be as specific as possible as you consider these questions:

How does this true north impact my family life?

How does this true north impact my work, if applicable?

How does this true north impact my school, if applicable?

How does this true north impact my health?

How does this true north impact my spiritual life, if applicable?

How does this true north impact my finances?

How does this true north impact my relationships with friends?

How does this true north impact my social life?

How does this true north impact me?

Your true north is something that guides all aspects of your life, not just certain components. If you've found yourself having a hard time answering some of these questions with the true north that you've landed on, go back and dig deeper.

If you're struggling to figure it out on your own, ask some friends, family members, or coworkers whom you trust - those who will tell you the truth, not the ones who are going to tell you want to hear. Ask them, "In what you've observed or learned about me in the time we've known each other, what is the one thing you think I could not live without? What is the one thing that I hold in the highest regard?" They might not hit the nail on the head, but they'll be able to give you some new insights to consider.

Ideas for action:

Observe Your Life

Today's Date: _____

The Hawthorne Effect is based on a study a company did with their employees in the 1920s. In the study, the company adjusted aspects of the physical environment to see what impact it would have on productivity. They found that it wasn't so much about the lighting or the way things were arranged, but more so that the employees were being observed. The act of being watched is what improved their productivity.

This study points out so clearly that, when you observe things, those things improve. For example, if you want to improve your eating habits, you should keep a diary of what you're consuming. Then, the facts are right in front of you to notice the reality of your diet. When you get a craving for ice cream because you haven't had it all week, you can look to your diary for the facts. You'll realize that even though you haven't had ice cream in three days, you did, in fact, have a piece of cake last night and a cookie the night before. You are actually having a sweet every night. I'm not saying that's good or bad. I'm simply saying that bringing that food diary into the equation allows you to observe your own behavior and the reality of the choices you are making.

Now, I want to be clear that no single action can equate to who you are as a human. These upcoming activities are not an opportunity to shame yourself or feel guilty about your life. Rather, they are an opportunity to see what is right in front of you. How can you improve if you don't know where you are?

It's time to take off the blinders, leave denial behind, and step into the reality of your current life. The next four activities are a measure of various aspects of your life. In defining your future, you must first get real with yourself about your current existence.

Before you take this next step, take a moment to recommit to yourself. Not only are the next activities exposing, lengthy, and confronting, but you may be tempted to stop the work here because the activities get too hard or take too much time. Take a moment to review your intentions on page 22 and your plan on page 19. Consider the following questions:

What progress have I already made toward my initial intentions?

To what degree am I committed to the plan that I created for myself?

Where is my commitment lacking in this journey?

What adjustments or additions do I need to make in order to continue doing this work?

Complete these sentences:

I want to show myself _____

_____.

Starting today, I will _____

_____.

TIP: Check in with the person you told about your plan in part one. Share with them the success you've experienced and the challenges you've faced. Share your recommitment and ask for accountability.

TIP: Commit one week to completing each of the below audits. Doing more than one at a time does not allow the space for deep learning and can be overwhelming.

Time Audit

Today's Date: _____

Now that you've identified what is most important to you, it's time to get real about how your current behaviors align. A time audit is a great tool to capture how you're spending your time. You might think you don't have enough time or that you're maximizing it to your benefit. In either case, this exercise will provide a true measure of what is accurate.

For the next week, use the following chart to document how you are spending your time. You'll notice that it is broken into 15-minute increments to get a true sense of the nitty-gritty, not just the big picture. Be as specific as possible with your activity. Instead of listing "family time," specify "Alicia's soccer game" or "Antonio's play." Instead of "relax," specify "movie" or "nap."

A single day may not be a true representation, but seven days will capture an overall average daily picture from which you can learn. While it's not recommended to do your time audit while on vacation, you do not need to wait for the most average week either. This activity is about what you can learn about how you spend your time rather than getting the picture exactly right. While it is impossible for this activity not to immediately influence how you're spending your time, try your best to resist adjusting your behavior during the audit so that you can get an accurate representation.

As you prepare for your time audit, take a moment to consider these questions:

What hypothesis do I want to make about how I'm spending my time?

What do I hope to learn through this activity?

What's my current relationship with time?

	Monday	Tuesday	Wednesday	Thursday	Friday	Saturday	Sunday
12:00 am							
12:15 am							
12:30 am							
12:45 am							
1:00 am							
1:15 am							
1:30 am							
1:45 am							
2:00 am							
2:15 am							
2:30 am							
2:45 am							
3:00 am							
3:15 am							
3:30 am							
3:45 am							
4:00 am							
4:15 am							
4:30 am							
4:45 am							
5:00 am							
5:15 am							
5:30am							
5:45 am							

	Monday	Tuesday	Wednesday	Thursday	Friday	Saturday	Sunday
6:00 am							
6:15 am							
6:30 am							
6:45 am							
7:00 am							
7:15 am							
7:30 am							
7:45 am							
8:00 am							
8:15 am							
8:30 am							
8:45 am							
9:00 am							
9:15 am							
9:30 am							
9:45 am							
10:00 am							
10:15 am							
10:30 am							
10:45 am							
11:00 am							
11:15 am							
11:30 am							
11:45 am							

	Monday	Tuesday	Wednesday	Thursday	Friday	Saturday	Sunday
12:00 pm							
12:15 pm							
12:30 pm							
12:45 pm							
1:00 pm							
1:15 pm							
1:30 pm							
1:45 pm							
2:00 pm							
2:15 pm							
2:30 pm							
2:45 pm							
3:00 pm							
3:15 pm							
3:30 pm							
3:45 pm							
4:00 pm							
4:15 pm							
4:30 pm							
4:45 pm							
5:00 pm							
5:15 pm							
5:30 pm							
5:45 pm							

	Monday	Tuesday	Wednesday	Thursday	Friday	Saturday	Sunday
6:00 pm							
6:15 pm							
6:30 pm							
6:45 pm							
7:00 pm							
7:15 pm							
7:30 pm							
7:45 pm							
8:00 pm							
8:15 pm							
8:30 pm							
8:45 pm							
9:00 pm							
9:15 pm							
9:30 pm							
9:45 pm							
10:00 pm							
10:15 pm							
10:30 pm							
10:45 pm							
11:00 pm							
11:15 pm							
11:30 pm							
11:45 pm							

Now that you've completed your time audit, categorize how much time you're spending doing each of the following things. Once you've totaled the number of hours in each category, divide by 168 (the number of hours in each week) and multiply by 100 to determine the percentage of each week you spend engaging in each activity.

Category	Hours	%	Category	Hours	%
Commute	___ / 168 x 100 = ___		Relaxation	___ / 168 x 100 = ___	
Dressing	___ / 168 x 100 = ___		School	___ / 168 x 100 = ___	
Errands	___ / 168 x 100 = ___		Sleep	___ / 168 x 100 = ___	
Exercise	___ / 168 x 100 = ___		Spouse Time	___ / 168 x 100 = ___	
Family Time	___ / 168 x 100 = ___		Work	___ / 168 x 100 = ___	
Friend Time	___ / 168 x 100 = ___		Other: _____	___ / 168 x 100 = ___	
Fun	___ / 168 x 100 = ___		Other: _____	___ / 168 x 100 = ___	
Meals	___ / 168 x 100 = ___		Other: _____	___ / 168 x 100 = ___	

Take a moment to consider these questions:

What was true about my original hypothesis? Why?

What wasn't quite right about my original hypothesis? Why?

What do I notice about how I'm wasting time?

What do I notice about how I'm leveraging time to my advantage?

How am I using time to align with my intentions?

What am I learning about my relationship with time?

What relationship do I want to have with time? Why?

How does my true north influence my relationship with time?

What am I learning about myself through this activity?

Ideas for action:

TIP: You can also conduct a work time audit to get a clear picture of your responsibilities in order to advocate for a promotion or set healthy boundaries.

TIP: This might be a great moment to revisit the Wheel of Emotions on page 26.

Money Audit

Today's Date: _____

When I was in college, a good friend of mine turned me on to Suze Orman, the female money maven. I faithfully watched her weekly show and listened to her podcast for years before finally purchasing one of her books. I don't recall all the steps in *The Nine Steps to Financial Freedom*,[2] but I do remember the third step was the most eye-opening. It has had the most influential and long-lasting impact on how I manage my money.

By the time I had purchased the book, I was in graduate school and was pinching every penny - or so I thought. She had me pulling out all my bank statements from the last 12 months - checking, savings, investments, retirement, everything. Now, in graduate school, I didn't really have investments or retirement, but I did balance my checking and savings accounts every single month.

I pulled out the last 12 months of statements and started sifting, categorizing, analyzing, and confronting. Indeed, I was not pinching every penny I had. In fact, I wasn't pinching pennies at all! I was spending left and right on eating out and drinks with friends. Each time I would go out, I would justify it by eating dinner at home and only going out for dessert or only getting one drink instead of five. Nevertheless, even these small purchases were adding up, and they were adding up to A LOT.

This activity will allow you to confront your beliefs - both true and false - about how you're managing your money. As you prepare for your money audit, take a moment to consider these questions:

What hypothesis do I want to make about how I spend money?

---

[2] Orman, Suze. (200g). *The 9 Steps to financial freedom: Practical and spiritual steps so you can stop worrying.* Currency

What do I hope to learn through this activity?

What's my current relationship with money?

Pull out the last twelve months of financial statements - every single penny coming in and going out. Don't skip a single charge. Don't skip a single deposit. Most banks make available the last 12 months of statements in your online account if you don't have print copies.

Compile every charge and every deposit into the first four columns of the chart below. You will likely need a separate notebook or some loose-leaf sheets of paper. You can also do this in a digital spreadsheet so it's easier to manipulate and use in the future. Download a sample spreadsheet by scanning the QR code here or by visiting www.lifelivedbydesign.com/money-audit.

Company/Organization/ Store	Amount Charged (Going Out)	Amount Deposited (Coming In)	Balance	Category

Once you've accounted for every penny coming in and going out over the last year, fill in the final column by classifying each purchase into the categories below. Some examples are provided for each category, though they are not exhaustive.

- **Children** - daycare, school tuition, extracurricular fees, babysitting
- **Clothes** - casual clothes, work clothes, undergarments, formal wear, shoes, hats
- **Connection Services** - cell phone, landline, internet
- **Eating Out** - restaurants, fast food, that grocery store run so you can bring a seven-layer dip to the party
- **Entertainment** - movies, concerts, bowling, sporting events, attractions, museums
- **Groceries & Essentials** - food to cook meals at home, cleaning supplies, home necessities
- **Hobbies & Habits** - outdoor equipment, craft materials, cost of collections, sports equipment, video gaming equipment, books, alcohol, tobacco, lottery tickets
- **Housing** - rent, mortgage payment, property taxes, regular maintenance, homeowners' association fees
- **Major Purchases** - televisions, phone, computer, kitchen appliances, home repairs, car repairs beyond regular maintenance
- **Medical** - insurance premiums, copays, medication, hospital visits
- **Pets** - food, treats, medical bills, toys, medication
- **Self-Care** - haircuts, manicures, pedicures, massages, facials, gym membership, coaching fees
- **Travel** - airline tickets, hotels, car rentals, gas for travel, campgrounds, train tickets
- **Utilities** - electric, water, sewer, gas
- **Vehicle** - lease or loan payment, gas for commute and daily errands, parking fees, insurance, oil change, tires, other regular maintenance
- **Other** - taxes, bank fees, interest payments, gifts (If you purchase a lot of gifts, you may want to separate this category.)

Finally, total your spending in each category and list them below:

Children	_____	Major Purchases	_____
Clothes	_____	Medical	_____
Connection Services	_____	Pets	_____
Eating Out	_____	Self-Care	_____
Entertainment	_____	Travel	_____
Groceries & Essentials	_____	Utilities	_____
Hobbies & Habits	_____	Vehicle	_____
Housing	_____	Other	_____

Take a moment to consider these questions:

What was true about my original hypothesis? Why?

What wasn't quite right about my original hypothesis? Why?

How am I wasting money?

How am I leveraging my financial situation to my benefit?

What am I learning about my relationship with money?

What relationship do I want to have with money? Why?

How does my true north influence my relationship with money?

If I share money responsibilities with a partner or spouse, how does that relationship impact how money is spent? How it's earned?

If I share money responsibilities with a partner or spouse, how does money impact that relationship?

What am I learning about myself through this activity?

TIP: The next time you question whether you should buy something, consider converting the monetary value to time. For example, if your hourly wage is US$11 (the average hourly wage in the US in February 2020[3]) and the item costs US$55, you would have to work 5 hours in order to earn the money to purchase that item. Is it worth it? If you are a salaried employee, divide your annual salary by 50 weeks (most employers offer salary employed at least two weeks vacation/sick leave) and again by 40 hours (even if you work more). This will give you a useful hourly wage to leverage.

TIP: This might be a great moment to revisit the Wheel of Emotions on page 26.

---

[3] Duffin, Erin. (2020, November 13). *Real average hourly earnings for all employees in the United States from October 2019 to October 2020.* Statista. Retrieved November 14, 2020, from https://www.statista.com/statistics/216259/monthly-real-average-hourly-earnings-for-all-employees-in-the-us/

Food Audit

Today's Date: _____

What you put in your body has a large impact on how you show up in life. This activity is not about eating healthy or associating your food intake with your weight. Instead, it's simply to acknowledge what you put into your body, what your thoughts are about it, and what feelings are evoked by that inner dialogue.

You may be a picky eater who eats out regularly and who doesn't enjoy vegetables. (I may or may not be talking about myself with that one.) If your inner dialogue about that is one that serves you and you experience positive feelings as a result, great! I'm not advocating that you change your habits simply to eat healthy, but rather to eat in a manner that contributes to your overall satisfaction in life. This is not meant to be shaming or guilt-ridden, but rather to shed light on your current habits. As a result, you can make more intentional and informed decisions about what foods are best for you. As you prepare for your food audit, take a moment to consider these questions:

What hypothesis do I want to make about what I put in my body?

What do I hope to learn through this activity?

What's my current relationship with food?

Over the next week, utilize this chart to document every food and drink item you take into your body. It may be helpful to utilize a separate journal for this activity for more space.

Food or Drink Item	What was my inner dialogue just before I chose to eat or drink this item?	How did I feel immediately after eating or drinking this item?	How did I feel one hour after eating or drinking this item?

Food or Drink Item	What was my inner dialogue just before I chose to eat or drink this item?	How did I feel immediately after eating or drinking this item?	How did I feel one hour after eating or drinking this item?

Food or Drink Item	What was my inner dialogue just before I chose to eat or drink this item?	How did I feel immediately after eating or drinking this item?	How did I feel one hour after eating or drinking this item?

Take a moment to consider these questions:

What was true about my original hypothesis? Why?

What wasn't quite right about my original hypothesis? Why?

What am I learning about my relationship with food?

What relationship do I want to have with food?

How does my true north influence my relationship with food?

What am I learning about myself through this activity?

Ideas for action:

TIP: This might be a great moment to revisit the Wheel of Emotions on page 26.

Relationship Audit

Today's Date: _____

You've probably heard the concept that you are a combination of those with whom you have the closest relationships. These are the people in your life who have the largest opportunity to support, challenge, push, and pull you along your journey. Whether you realize it or not, you give a lot of power to the people with whom you are closest. Just as with your time, money, and eating habits, it's time to have a frank conversation with yourself about your inner circle. As you prepare for your relationship audit, take a moment to consider these questions:

What hypothesis do I want to make about my inner circle?

What do I hope to learn through this activity?

The 5 people (family or friends) who I consider my strongest relationships are:

	Name	What value do I provide them? How do I pour into them?	What value do they provide me? How do they pour into me?
1			
2			
3			
4			
5			

The last 20 people to whom I sent a text or from whom I received a text are: (Do not duplicate names. If you have a group text in your top 20, count each of those people individually.)

	Name	What value do I provide them? How do I pour into them?	What value do they provide me? How do they pour into me?
1			
2			
3			
4			
5			
6			

	Name	What value do I provide them? How do I pour into them?	What value do they provide me? How do they pour into me?
7			
8			
9			
10			
11			
12			
13			

	Name	What value do I provide them? How do I pour into them?	What value do they provide me? How do they pour into me?
14			
15			
16			
17			
18			
19			
20			

The last 5 people that I called or who called me are: (Do not count companies or businesses.)

	Name	What value do I provide them? How do I pour into them?	What value do they provide me? How do they pour into me?
1			
2			
3			
4			
5			

Take a moment to consider these questions:

Of the people I listed above who are not my family members, if I met each of them for the first time today, who would I choose to befriend? Why?

Of the people I listed above who are my family members, if they were not my family members, who would I choose to keep in my life moving forward? Why?

What is true about my original hypothesis? Why?

What isn't quite right about my original hypothesis? Why?

What did I notice within myself as I was writing each name on these lists?

What did my gut tell me as I went through this activity?

What was my inner dialogue as I completed this activity?

What am I learning about my inner circle?

How does my true north influence my relationships?

What am I learning about myself through this activity?

Ideas for action:

Resentment & Fear

Today's Date: _____

To resent someone is "to feel or express annoyance or ill will at."[4] You can resent someone for any number of reasons (e.g., something they did or said to you, something they didn't do or say to you, something they have that you don't, a misperception of who they are, etc.).

This activity illuminates the connection between your resentment and your fears. When you examine these resentful relationships, you learn that the reasons why you resent someone is typically associated with an underlying fear. For example, you may be resentful towards a coworker who is always trying to get you in trouble. If you do in fact get in trouble, you could lose your job, which would result in no income and other financial implications. Your resentment towards your coworker may be connected to your fear of financial insecurity.

Once you have identified this, you can then take it a step further to better understand how you can mitigate this fear. For example, let's say the way your coworker is trying to get you in trouble is by calling you out each time you are even one minute late. You can then mitigate the underlying fear by showing up on time or even 5 minutes early. You see, there is always something that you can own within each of these relationships in order to take your power back and reduce your fear.

Take a look at the connections between your resentment and fears by identifying your resentful relationships first. The more thorough your list is the more insights you will gain, so consider your current and past relationships. I recommend shooting for at least 20 names on this list. You may have 100 or more when you look at every relationship over the course of your lifetime including family, friends, teachers, coaches, friends' families, neighbors, coworkers, mentors, community leaders, etc. Be as thorough as you need to be to glean insights in the follow-up reflection questions.

---

[4] resent. 2020. In Merriam-Webster.com. Retrieved November 14, 2020, from https://www.merriam-webster.com/dictionary/resent

Name of the person I resent.	Why do I resent this person?	What fear is being triggered by this resentment?	How can I mitigate this fear as it relates to this person?

Name of the person I resent.	Why do I resent this person?	What fear is being triggered by this resentment?	How can I mitigate this fear as it relates to this person?

Once you feel your list is thorough enough to glean insights, review the third column where you listed your fears associated with the resentment. Typically, three to four common fears will begin to show up over and over. They may manifest in different forms of resentment, but there tends to be less than a handful of common fears underlying your resentment.

What are my common fears?

_____   _____

_____   _____

Take a moment to consider these questions:

What is resentment trying to teach me?

How are these fears holding me back?

What happens when I acknowledge the fear without embracing it?

What am I learning about myself through this activity?

Ideas for action:

TIP: If you have no fears, you will have no resentment; therefore, the key to reducing or eliminating resentment in your relationships is to address the underlying fears head on.

TIP: This might be a great moment to revisit the Wheel of Emotions on page 26.

Your Priority

Today's Date: _____

Who is your #1 priority? Is it your kids? Your spouse? Your significant other? Maybe it's your employer? Maybe your parents or a parent? I don't mean who you want your #1 priority to be or who you think your #1 priority is. I mean for you to dig deep and ask yourself who is your #1 priority? Who is the one person that you make time for every single day? Not just, "Oh I spend time with them every day, or I spend time for them every single day," but "I make time for this person because they are that important to me."

I'm here to tell you if that person is not yourself, you've got some work to do. The single most important relationship in your life is the one you have with yourself. I'm not telling you to be a selfish person. What I am saying is that you need to have selfish moments every single day.

Take a moment to consider these questions:

How do I treat myself?

How do I talk to myself?

How do I embrace my emotions?

How do I honor my wishes?

How do I respect myself?

How do I take care of myself?

How do I express gratitude toward myself?

Would I allow a friend, my best friend, or a stranger to treat me the way I treat myself? Why or why not?

What am I learning about myself through this activity?

Ideas for action:

Negative Nancy

Today's Date: _____

Have you ever been around someone who constantly complains? Someone who never seems to have anything positive to say, despite having plenty of great things happening in their life? It's exhausting being around these types of people. You can probably imagine how draining it is to live in a state of perpetual dread and negativity and with a glass-completely-empty attitude.

While you may not personally experience negativity to this degree, it is natural for you to complain at times. Sometimes you get caught in a complaint cycle without even realizing it. For many, one of the triggers for complaining is comparison.

When you compare yourself to those around you, it opens two possibilities: (1) comparison that inspires action, or (2) comparison that is debilitating to you. Comparing your life to those around you is not inherently bad. It is, however, inherently human. The key is to compare in service to yourself - to compare in a manner that drives you towards action rather than paralyzes your thoughts and puts you in a space of complaining.

For example, I have a good friend who travels internationally significantly more than I do. I could look at their pictures and compare my travels in a way that creates the thought, "Must be nice. Look at you and all your fancy vacations." Or, I could look at them with aspirational thoughts such as, "I can't wait to go there. When I make it to Fiji, I'm going to get all of my tips from them first." You can see how one version of these thoughts serves me and one does not.

This reflection is meant to shed light on some of your most common complaints to illuminate a different way of considering them.

Take a moment to consider these questions:

What parts of my day do I most dread? What are my inner thoughts about this?

What parts of my week do I most dread? What are my inner thoughts about this?

What parts of the year do I most dread? What are my inner thoughts about this?

What parts of my job do I most dread? What are my inner thoughts about this?

Which friendships do I find most challenging? What are my inner thoughts about this?

Which family members do I struggle to connect with? What are my inner thoughts about this?

What aspects of my life cause me the most stress? What are my inner thoughts about this?

Who do I perceive as having a "better" life than me? What are my inner thoughts about this?

How am I comparing myself to others in ways that are not serving me? What are my inner thoughts about this?

What am I learning about myself through this activity?

Once you've taken time to become so familiar with your inner thoughts that you can quote yourself, return to each of these responses and consider an alternative thought that is more useful or constructive. For example, I once took a job that didn't get me any closer to my professional goals and had a less than collaborative team. It was challenging to show up with a positive attitude each day. However, once I created a daily reminder that this job is getting me closer to my financial goals on a much quicker timeline, I was able to show up in a more productive manner. Where can you put your focus in each of the above situations so they can be leveraged toward your true north?

Ideas for action:

Your Inner Critic

Today's Date: _____

You've probably noticed that you've spent a good amount of time recognizing your inner dialogue. How you talk to yourself has a direct impact on how you behave and the subsequent results you experience. It is a natural part of life for some of this inner dialogue to be negative thoughts that do not serve you well, but there's also a deeper voice that shows up consistently, over-time, and across many situations. This voice extends beyond negative thoughts and influences your negative beliefs and negative perspectives on your life. It is your inner critic. This activity is designed to help you confront your inner critic and reassign its responsibilities.

When things are not going well, what kinds of things do I say to myself?

What else do I tell myself? Be specific and use quotes. What are the actual words I say to myself?

What's the core message I keep coming back to?

If a small character were to appear on this page saying these things to me, what would it look like? Utilize the open space to draw or collage a picture of this small character. Consider the following questions as you draw or collage:

- What is the small character wearing?
- What is the expression on the small character's face?
- What color is this small character?
- What is the small character doing?

Once you have a clear image of your small, inner critic character, take a moment to consider these questions:

What name do I want to give this small character?

When does this small character show up most often?

What are they after when they show up?

What trait within me is this small character testing? Why?

How do I want to handle this small character when it appears?

Who would I be without this small character?

What am I learning about myself through this activity?

Ideas for action:

To see what my inner critic looks like, scan the QR code here or visit www.lifelivedbydesign.com/inner-critic.

TIP: Pay close attention to when your small character shows up in the next week. Increasing awareness of your negative thoughts helps set you up to successfully reframe them to thoughts that serve you.

TIP: This might be a great moment to revisit the Wheel of Emotions on page 26.

Personal 360° Review

Today's Date: _____

360° reviews have been leveraged in the corporate world for many years. Within a company, the purpose is to receive feedback from all stakeholders, not just from a supervisor. These surveys are sent to supervisors, peers, employees, and sometimes vendors and customers. The purpose is to get closer to a more full perspective of individual and company-wide strengths and opportunities for growth.

In this workbook, a twist is being put on this idea to make it more personal. This is your opportunity to receive feedback from a wide variety of people in your life. You will be connecting with those whom you have varied relationships (e.g. friends, family, coworkers, mentors, community leaders, etc.) to receive their feedback.

Learning About Yourself

First, choose the questions you want to include in your survey. You don't want to choose only questions that will simply boost you up and you also don't want to choose only questions that will make you feel down. Be sure to select a good mix that will provide you with deeper insights about yourself. It's recommended that you choose between 5-7 questions. This will give you enough information from which you can glean themes, but not too many questions that it will discourage your reviewers from completing the survey. Here are some questions to get you started:

1. What are my greatest strengths?
2. What are some of my blindspots?
3. How can I be a better friend/sibling/spouse/coworker/family member to you?
4. How do I get in my own way?
5. How can I step into leadership?
6. How do I make you feel?
7. How would you describe my energy?

8. What internal dialogue do you have about me?

9. What potential am I overlooking?

10. How do I handle mistakes?

11. How adaptable and flexible am I?

12. What is my relationship with boundaries?

13. How well do I manage my emotions?

14. How well do I handle adversity?

15. What do you notice about my ability to take risks?

16. What do you notice about my ability to follow through?

17. How do I receive feedback (both positive and constructive)?

18. What do you notice about how I interact with others?

19. What do you notice about how I handle conflict?

20. How do I handle change?

21. What else would you like to share?

Identifying Reviewers

Consider family, close friends, acquaintances, coworkers, community leaders, and mentors. Remember, this is meant to be a learning opportunity, so you want to consider those people who will be honest with compassion. You will probably receive responses from no more than half the people on this list. While you can certainly include more than ten people in your life, I challenge you to think of at least ten people in an effort to provide you with diverse perspectives and enough responses to allow you to draw out themes. This is just to get you started.

1. _____

2. _____

3. _____

4. _____

5. _____

6. _____

7. _____

8. _____

9. _____

10. _____

Sending the Survey

There are many ways to distribute the survey. The single, most important piece is that all the feedback is anonymous. You should not be asking any questions about the person's name, email address, relationship to you, or any other identifiers. The purpose of the anonymity is two-fold: (1) it creates a space that increases the comfort of those who are providing feedback to be as honest as possible, and (2) it encourages you to focus on the feedback rather than the person giving the feedback. The best way to ensure anonymity is to have someone else send the survey on your behalf and collect the responses for you. This activity is not about who gave you what feedback, but rather what themes show up in the compiled responses and what insights you can gain. These themes and insights will help you grow further along your journey of knowing all aspects of yourself.

There are several free, online survey platforms such as SurveyMonkey, Google Forms, or JotForm. You can also print copies of the survey to provide to your reviewers, so long as all responses are kept anonymous.

Regardless of whether you create an online survey or a print survey, you will want to include an explanation. Let your reviewers know about the work you're doing, what you're hoping to gain from the feedback, and information about confidentiality. Here's an example email or letter you can include:

Hi Heather,

I hope this message finds you doing well! I am on a bold journey of knowing myself, and I've already learned so much. I also know that the work of self-discovery can't happen without including the perspective of those whose opinions I value most. You have had an impact on my life, and as I continue on this journey, I'd love to hear some honest, transparent feedback from you. I've put together 5 simple questions for you to share your thoughts anonymously. Knowing how others perceive me is an important part in the process of knowing myself, and I appreciate any amount of time and energy you are willing to offer in the next two weeks in sharing your perspective. I plan to review and reflect on all the anonymous feedback on [date]. Thank you for always being someone I can count on to challenge me to do more and to be more.

Take care,

Brittany

Use this space to write your own message that will be sent with your survey.

Preparing for Responses

While it may be tempting to take a peek at the responses as they come in, remember, it's not about who said what, but rather what themes emerge from the overall feedback. With this in mind, choose a date (I recommend about two weeks from when you send the survey) to sit down, review, and reflect on the feedback in totality. Carve out about an hour of uninterrupted time to delve into making meaning from the thoughts that were shared with you.

I will review my feedback on _____ at _____.

In the time between sending the survey and reviewing the responses, you may experience any number of emotions - excitement, anxiety, nervousness, anger. Revisit the Wheel of Emotions on page 26 before you open the survey responses and take a moment to consider these questions:

What is the internal dialogue I am experiencing as I wait for the responses?

What emotions are present for me as I think about receiving feedback?

How do I make meaning from these emotions?

Who do I want to be as I review this feedback?

How do I receive positive feedback?

How do I receive negative feedback?

What do I hope to learn about myself through this process?

Making Meaning

On the date and time you chose above, take a moment to review your previous reflections and check in with yourself before reviewing the responses.

What is present for me right now as I am about to open the responses?

Read through the responses from those who completed your 360° survey. Remember that this is an opportunity for learning and growth. Try to resist the urge to identify who said what as you consider these questions.

What jumps out at me in the responses? Why does that jump out?

What surprises me? Why does that surprise me?

What themes emerge from the responses?

What parts of the feedback do I agree with? Why?

What parts of the feedback cause me discomfort? Why?

Where are the opportunities for growth?

What is the biggest misconception others have of me?

What am I learning about myself through this activity?

Ideas for action:

Recommitment

Today's Date: _____

Receiving feedback from those whom you respect, admire, and trust can be confronting, enlightening, exposing, exciting, and any number of other emotions. It creates space for you to kick your feet up out of satisfaction, quit due to resistance, or dig in deeper for additional growth and learning. I encourage you to choose the latter of these options. Take a moment to recommit yourself to this bold journey.

In what ways am I giving a half-hearted effort to this work?

In what ways am I all in on this work?

Who do I need to be to continue on this bold journey?

Complete these sentences:

I want to prove to myself _____

_____.

Starting today, I will _____

_____.

TIP: Check in with the person you told about your plan in part one. Share with them the success you've experienced and the challenges you've faced. Share your recommitment and ask for accountability.

Personal Well-being

Today's Date: _____

Carol Ryff[5] developed the six-factor model of psychological well-being, which identifies the main indicators of well-being. Ryff defines each of these as follows:

- **Self-Acceptance**: has a "positive attitude toward self; acknowledges and accepts multiple aspects of self, including good and bad qualities; feels positive about past life"

- **Purpose in Life**: has "goals in life and a sense of directness; feels there is meaning to present and past life; holds beliefs that give life purpose; has aims and objectives for living"

- **Environmental Mastery**: has a "sense of mastery and competence in managing the environment; controls complex array of external activities; makes effective use of surrounding opportunities; able to choose or create contexts suitable to personal needs and values"

- **Positive Relationships**: has "warm, satisfying, trusting relationships with others; concerned about the welfare of others; capable of strong empathy, affection, and intimacy; understands give-and-take of human relationships"

- **Personal Growth**: has a "feeling of continued development; sees self as growing and expanding; open to new experiences; sense of realizing potential; sees improvement in self and behavior over time; changing in ways that reflect more self-knowledge and effectiveness"

- **Autonomy**: has the ability to be "self-determining and independent; able to resist social pressures to think and act in certain ways; regulates behavior from within; evaluates self by personal standards"

This exercise allows space to consider your personal well-being and your level of mastery within each of these six factors.

1. Consider your level of mastery in each wedge independently. Give it a score of 1-10, where 1 is "I'm a beginner," and 10 is "I've mastered this." It's important to consider your current level of

5 Ryff, Carol D. (1995). Psychological Well-Being in Adult Life. *Current Directions in Psychological Science, 4*(4), 99-104. https://lemosandcrane.co.uk/resources/RISE%20psychological%20wellbeing%20in%20adulthood.pdf

mastery today, not where you'd like it to be. Write your rating next to each category on your wheel.

2. Shade in the wheel to represent the number you gave the respective wedge to provide more visual clarity of your snapshot.

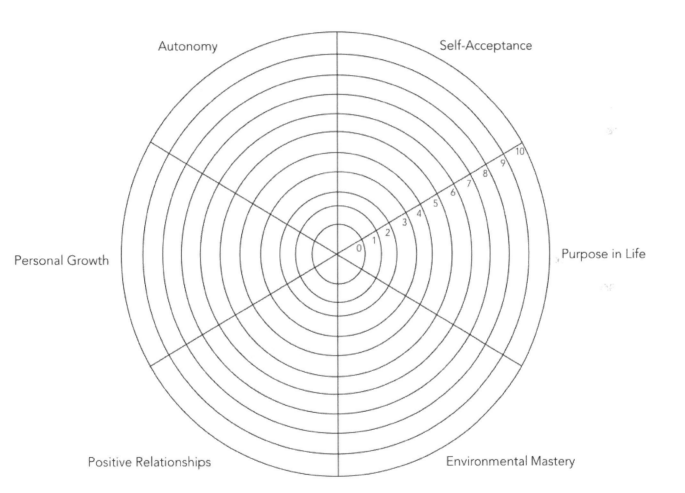

Take a moment to consider these questions:

Other than the numbers themselves, what jumps out at me about my personal well-being? Why does that jump out at me right now?

What surprises me about my personal well-being? Why does that surprise me?

What do I notice about some connections between the different factors of my personal well-being?

Who am I when I am doing well?

Who am I when I'm not doing well?

What am I learning about myself through this activity?

Ideas for action:

When Things Go Well

Today's Date: _____

"Change is inevitable. Growth is optional." John C. Maxwell

Change is going to happen whether you welcome it or not. You do, however, have control over whether or not you grow through that change. Are you the one that, as these waves of change are coming, you ride the wave and it's gone? Do you just float around waiting for the next wave of change to happen to you? Do you hope you don't drown in the process?

Or, are you taking advantage of the waves and preparing yourself for them? Are you confronting them head-on ready to swim and use the momentum of the wave to get you closer to where you want to go? Are you leveraging change as an opportunity for learning and growth and taking control of the impact on your life?

The latter scenario should be the case whether you are growing through positive waves of change or not so positive waves of change. It's easy to be critical of yourself when things are not going the way you would like for them to go. It's also important to be observant when things are going well. Recognizing your contribution to the outcomes in your life when it's going well can serve you immensely for when things take a turn. Knowing who you are in good times can help you leverage that mindset to pull yourself out of times that aren't so great.

This activity is designed to help you capture perspectives from moments in your life when things were going well. Once these perspectives are identified, you can actively shift into them in moments where they might serve you in the future.

Perspective One

When was a time that I felt carefree? Be as specific as possible in recalling this moment. Put myself in that moment again. What was happening?

What was I feeling in this carefree moment?

What was my mindset in this carefree moment?

Who was I when I was there?

What was my energy like in this carefree moment?

What else do I want to add so I remember this carefree perspective?

If this carefree perspective was a color, what color would it be?

What two to three-word name could I give this perspective?

Perspective Two

When was a time that I was bold? Be as specific as possible in recalling this moment. Put myself in that moment again. What was happening?

What emotions does this bold moment evoke for me?

What kind of things do I say to myself in this bold perspective?

Who was I when I was there?

What was my energy like in this bold moment?

What else do I want to add so I remember this bold perspective?

If this bold perspective were an animal, what animal would it be?

What two to three-word name could I give this perspective?

Perspective Three

When was a time that I felt fulfilled? Be as specific as possible in recalling this moment. Put myself in that moment again. What was happening?

What gave me that fulfillment?

What was my mindset in this fulfilled moment?

Who was I when I was there?

What was my energy like in this fulfilled moment?

What else do I want to add so I remember this fulfilled perspective?

If this fulfilled perspective was a form of transportation, what form of transportation would it be?

What two to three-word name could I give this perspective?

Perspective Four

When was a time that I felt authentic? Be as specific as possible in recalling this moment. Put myself in that moment again. What was happening?

What was I feeling in this authentic moment?

What was my attitude in this authentic moment?

What strengths was I drawing on in this authentic moment?

What was my energy like in this authentic moment?

What else do I want to add so I remember this authentic perspective?

If this authentic perspective were a place in the world, what place in the world would it be?

What two to three-word name could I give this perspective?

Naming each of these perspectives helps make them sticky. Now that you have a more tangible way to recall the moments when things were going well, you can more easily access them in moments where you need them most.

List my four perspectives here:

_____   _____

_____   _____

Ideas for action:

TIP: Post the names of your perspectives in a place where you will see them when you need them most. For example, maybe you want to leverage your bold perspective at work, so you might write the name of that perspective on the cover of the notebook you use at work.

<u>Obligation Versus Responsibility</u>

Today's Date: _____

Why do you make the decisions that you make every single day? Why do you stay in that job? Why do you keep your relationship going with your partner or your spouse? Why do you stay connected with family members? Why do you go to church or temple or synagogue? Or why do you not do these things? Is it out of obligation or responsibility?

Interestingly enough, when you look at obligation and responsibility in the thesaurus, they are synonyms for one another. However, according to the Merriam-Webster dictionary they're quite different.

Obligation is "a debt of gratitude" or "something one is bound to do."[6] On the other hand, responsibility is "liable to be called on to answer. Being the cause or explanation. Able to answer for one's conduct. Able to choose for oneself between right and wrong."[7]

In other words, obligation is being held accountable to something outside yourself, such as your employer, your spouse, a family member, or societal expectations. While responsibility is being held accountable to yourself because you feel it's the right thing to do. Because you made a commitment to yourself. Because it is in alignment with your true north.

[6] obligation. 2020. In Merriam-Webster.com. Retrieved November 14, 2020, from https://www.merriam-webster.com/dictionary/obligation

[7] responsible. 2020. In Merriam-Webster.com. Retrieved November 14, 2020, from https://www.merriam-webster.com/dictionary/responsible

Take a moment to consider these questions:

How am I living an obligated life? Why?

How am I living a responsible life? Why?

What is the impact of each?

What kind of life do I want to live as it relates to obligation and responsibility? Why?

Who do I need to be to step more fully into that life?

What am I learning about myself through this activity?

Ideas for action:

Personal Agency

Today's Date: _____

In the context of positive psychology, agency is the ability to believe in yourself. It is the belief that you have the knowledge and resources to accomplish your intentions. This is a critical aspect of your bold journey. It creates hope for the future, a determination to persist, and that elusive character trait that so many strive for - confidence. Developing agency is not simple and it does not occur overnight, but it can be learned. When you have a strong belief in your own abilities, skills, and talents, you make more decisions based on your own personal vision rather than the vision that others have for you.

	How have my decisions in this area been influenced by outside factors?	How have my decisions in this area been influenced by my personal vision?
My chosen career		
Professional growth		
Personal growth		
Spiritual practice		

	How have my decisions in this area been influenced by outside factors?	How have my decisions in this area been influenced by my personal vision?
Development of friendships		
Relationships with immediate family		
Relationships with extended family		
Relationship with significant other		
Relationship with myself		
Financial earnings		
Financial spendings		

	How have my decisions in this area been influenced by outside factors?	How have my decisions in this area been influenced by my personal vision?
Financial savings		
Fun		
Personal education		
Physical health		
Emotional health		
Mental health		
Where I live		

	How have my decisions in this area been influenced by outside factors?	How have my decisions in this area been influenced by my personal vision?
How I live		
Why I live		

Take a moment to consider these questions:

To what degree do I trust myself?

To what degree am I living my life for others?

To what degree am I living my life for myself?

How do I want to live my life?

What do I want, simply because I want it?

What is possible if I doubled my personal agency?

What am I learning about myself through this activity?

Ideas for action:

TIP: This might be a great moment to revisit the Wheel of Emotions on page 26.

The Bigger Picture

Today's Date: _____

As you wrap up part two, look back over your reflections and notes from the activities thus far, and take a moment to reflect on these questions:

What themes am I seeing come to the surface through this examination of my life as it currently exists?

What has surprised me thus far? Why?

What emotions are coming up as I take inventory of my "here"?

What do I want to carry forward with me?

What do I need to let go of?

What is absolutely true about my life?

For that to be true, what has to be in place?

Ideas for action:

Brain Dump

Today's Date: _____

Whew! You made it! It's been an exploration that evoked a range of emotions and required a great deal of honesty and dedication on your part to get here. This work is hard and also extremely rewarding. You will reap the rewards of this work far beyond your time doing these activities, even if you stop here (although I hope you don't).

Before you shift gears from the present to the future, do another brain dump. Pull out a timer and set it for five minutes. Press start and use this space to free write for the entire time about what is present for you having completed part two of this workbook.

Don't worry about spelling, grammar, incomplete sentences, legibility, or even whether you stay on topic or not. Simply write whatever comes to mind in whatever order it comes. You may even decide to draw instead of write words or a combination of art and words. Whatever you choose, let the pen flow, let your thoughts flow, and don't stop until the timer sounds.

No one will be reading this except you and those with whom you choose to share it, so let your thoughts flow freely. The purpose of this activity is to capture the bigger picture of your experience in part two all in one place.

If you'd like a more pointed question, consider this: What's the point of all that I'm doing? What am I progressing toward?

Ready. Set. Go!

TIP: Before starting part three, take a break (no more than a week, so you don't lose momentum). You've done a lot of heavy lifting. Pat yourself on the back for remaining committed and celebrate this milestone. Return to page 19 to remind yourself of how you planned to celebrate getting to this point.

TIP: This is also a great time to play the vision recording you created for yourself before starting this work.

TIP: This might be a great moment to revisit the Wheel of Emotions on page 26.

Part Three: There

Live the life you love.

-Bob Marley

Brain Dump

Today's Date: _____

Before you begin defining what your future holds, let's take a moment to clear your brain of clutter. Pull out a timer and set it for five minutes. Press start and use this space to free write for the entire time. Don't worry about spelling, grammar, incomplete sentences, or legibility. Simply write whatever comes to mind in whatever order it comes. You may even decide to draw instead of write words or a combination of art and words. Whatever you choose, let the pen flow and don't stop until the timer sounds.

No one will be reading this except you and those with whom you choose to share it, so let your thoughts flow freely. The purpose of this activity is to declutter your mind, so you can be fully present with the activities in part three.

Ready. Set. Go!

<u>Empowering Assumptions</u>

Today's Date: _____

Before you step into creating a vision for your future, take a moment to tackle some of the assumptions you hold about what is possible for yourself. This activity is designed to help expose how your assumptions play a large role in the results you see in your life. You'll first do a negative cycle followed by a positive cycle.

In the negative cycle, it can be tempting to justify your thoughts or actions or to convince yourself that it's not that bad. Remember, there is no judgement in this process. Just as with all activities in this workbook, this too serves as an opportunity to shed light and learn about yourself. Try to resist the urge to push toward the positive, so you can learn about the true connection between your negative thoughts and the results to which they lead.

Before you dive into the two cycles, capture all the assumptions you hold about your future - both positive and negative. Try not to filter your thoughts. Simply make a list of all the assumptions you make about what is possible for your life.

O _____

O _____

O _____

O _____

O _____

O _____

O _____

O _____

O _____

O _____

O _____

O _____

O _____

O _____

O _____

O _____

O _____

In an effort to gain the most from this activity, take a moment to isolate and select just one of these assumption from the list above that is not serving you. You'll dig a bit deeper into this assumption Write that single assumption next to #1 in the chart on the next page and complete it in sequentia order.

1. What is my isolated assumption?

_____

_____

_____

2. When I make this negative assumption, what perspective does that put me in? What emotions does this assumption evoke in me? What energy do I feel when I say this assumption aloud? What mindset does this assumption put me in?

_____

_____

_____

_____

_____

_____

_____

_____

5. How do the results I listed in step 4 connect back to the original negative assumption?

_____

_____

_____

Negative Assumption

4. When I take the actions that I listed in step 3, what results do I typically see in my life?

_____

_____

_____

3. When I am experiencing the emotions, energy, attitude, and mindset I listed in step 2, what action do I typically take from that place?

_____

_____

_____

Take a moment to remember what it's like in this chart and then move on to the positive cycle.

Let's play with the original negative assumption to see what is possible. What is the exact opposite of the negative assumption you leveraged in the previous chart? This need not be an assumption you can whole-heartedly believe. You're just playing to see what can be learned. Write that single opposite assumption next to #1 and follow the sequential order again.

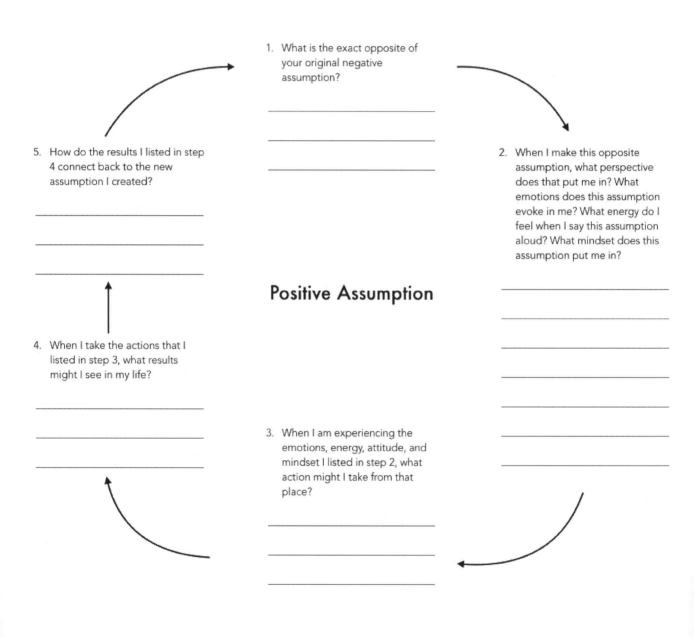

1. What is the exact opposite of your original negative assumption?

_____

_____

_____

2. When I make this opposite assumption, what perspective does that put me in? What emotions does this assumption evoke in me? What energy do I feel when I say this assumption aloud? What mindset does this assumption put me in?

_____

_____

_____

_____

_____

_____

5. How do the results I listed in step 4 connect back to the new assumption I created?

_____

_____

_____

Positive Assumption

4. When I take the actions that I listed in step 3, what results might I see in my life?

_____

_____

_____

3. When I am experiencing the emotions, energy, attitude, and mindset I listed in step 2, what action might I take from that place?

_____

_____

_____

Take a moment to consider these questions:

Which chart is more empowering for me? Why?

Who do I need to be to step into this chart more often?

What am I learning about what I can control in the two charts?

How are my assumptions holding me back from fully living the life I want to live?

How can I take more control over the life I lead?

What am I learning about who I am becoming through this activity?

Ideas for action:

TIP: Each assumption you make leads to a different perspective, which leads to different actions and results. For even deeper learning, take each negative assumption you listed on pages 169-170 through the chart to see what can be learned.

TIP: If the new assumption is absolutely impossible for you to begin shifting toward, consider a more neutral assumption as a stepping stone. For example, if your original assumption is "my supervisor is the worst" and you are having a hard time jumping to "my supervisor is the best," maybe more neutral ground is "I have a supervisor."

Your Past Is Irrelevant

Today's Date: _____

One of the absolute best parts of living an examined life is that your past does not determine your future - the way things have been does not mean that's the way they will be moving forward. Every day, you get to choose the life you want to live, the life you want to step into, the life you want to create for yourself.

In consideration of this perspective, take a moment to journal on this single prompt:

If my past is irrelevant, how do I define myself moving forward?

Meet Your Future Self

Today's Date: _____

It is a natural tendency for you to seek advice from others. It's a means of validating your beliefs, your opinions, your choices, and who you are. What if you could get advice from an older, more experienced, wiser version of yourself? This activity serves exactly this purpose.

How old will you be 10 years from now? _____

To meet your future self, scan the QR code here or visit www.lifelivedbydesign.com/future-self. Before pressing play, find a comfortable space - one where you will not be interrupted. Allow your imagination to lead the way. As you listen, try not to be so worried about seeing a clear scene. What is important is the learning that comes from this activity.

Notes:

Take a moment to consider these questions:

Where did I meet my future self?

What was happening in the scene where I met my future self?

What did my future self look like?

What was my reaction when I first saw my future self?

What stood out to me most about my future self? Why?

What surprised me about my future self? Why?

What energy did I feel from my future self?

What message did my future self have for me?

What would my future self say I still need to learn about myself? Why?

What was the hardest thing my future self had to overcome? What made it so difficult?

What would my future self say about who I am becoming?

What gift can I give my future self today?

What's the nickname by which I can call my future self?

How will I remember to call upon my future self when I most need advice?

What am I learning about who I am becoming through this activity?

Ideas for action:

<u>Looking Back, Looking Forward</u>

Today's Date: _____

This activity includes excerpts from Ryan Moran.[8] To watch the complete video, scan the QR code here or visit www.lifelivedbydesign.com/ryan-moran.

"I realized the other day that there are two sides to everything. There are the problems that we feel in the moment, and there are the positives that we think about in the rearview mirror. We feel the problems, and we long for the positives. We rarely, if ever, pause to appreciate the positives while we're still in them. And instead we just experience them later. And we experience them in the sense of missing the times that used to be."

"The beautiful curse about being human is that we are wired to find problems. That does not make us happy, it actually makes us miserable. But it also makes us grow and create and to solve those problems. We rarely, if ever, pause to appreciate the things that are in our life that we could be grateful for until it is too late. But you get to control what you focus on. You get to control whether you consciously appreciate things that are in your life, or if you focus on the problems and you wait until later when you feel that sense of longing for how things used to be."

"I can promise you there is someone else looking at your life longing to be in your situation, even in a situation that right now you see as a problem."

[8] Moran, Ryan. (2019, April 19). *As a kid all I ever wanted was to be a millionaire, and now I am. And yet, all I* [Video attached] [Status update]. Facebook. https://www.facebook.com/ryandanielmoran/posts/as-a-kid-all-i-ever-wanted-was-to-be-a-millionaire-and-now-i-amand-yet-all-i-wan/10156317229493310/

Take a moment to consider these questions:

What did I previously have in life that I currently long for?

What do I currently have in my life that I previously longed for?

Who did I have to be to bring that into my life?

What do I currently have in my life that my future self is longing for?

What does my future self have that I am currently longing for?

What are my current perceived problems? Why do I perceive these as problems?

What are these perceived problems trying to teach me? Why?

Five years from now, when these perceived problems are in the rearview mirror, what are the positive thoughts I will have about them?

How am I living in my past? Why?

What are the things I want to do "some day"? Why am I putting these off?

What would I long for most if it were taken away from me? Why?

What am I learning about who I am becoming through this activity?

Ideas for action:

Starting Over

Today's Date: _____

One way to consider what's possible is to start over. Imagine that you have an opportunity to capture everything you've learned to this point in your life, put it in a container, and start over from the day you were born with everything in that container. If you were to restart knowing everything you know today, what kind of life would you build for yourself? Utilize the space below to write or draw what comes to mind. Be as specific as possible.

Crazy, Wild Dreams

Today's Date: _____

Take this page to spell out your craziest, wildest dreams. If you had a magic wand to create any life you wanted, what would it include? You can draw, write, create a collage - whatever strikes your fancy. Be as detailed as possible and consider all aspects of your life - personal, professional, health, relationships, spirituality, finances, fun, and living circumstances.

Take a moment to consider these questions:

What was my inner dialogue as I was crafting my wildest, craziest dreams?

What held me back from dreaming even bigger? Why?

What limitations have I placed on my dreams? Why?

What limitations has society placed on my dreams? Why?

What is my deepest truth?

What do I long for? Why?

What do I crave more than anything? Why?

What's shining inside me beneath the noise and chatter?

What am I learning about who I am becoming through this activity?

Taking into consideration your reflections, utilize this space to dream EVEN BIGGER, WILDER, CRAZIER dreams for yourself.

TIP: This might be a great moment to revisit the Wheel of Emotions on page 26.

Developing Your Passions

Today's Date: _____

For a very long time, I would roll my eyes when I heard phrases like "find your passion" or "follow your passion" or "when you do what you're passionate about, it won't feel like work" or any other comments about passion that are supposed to be inspirational and encouraging. Rather than being encouraged by them, I would internally beat myself up. "Why can't I find my passion? They talk about it as if it's easy to find. I've been looking and nothing lights my heart on fire. Yes, there are things I enjoy, but nothing makes me jump out of bed in the morning eager to start my day."

I had completely given up on this idea of finding my passion and had accepted the fact that I probably wouldn't find true fulfillment in life because I wasn't getting any closer to my passion.

That is until I came across a new way of considering what passion is. The Latin root of the word passion is pati-, which means to suffer.[9] In essence, passion is what you are willing to suffer for or endure challenging times for.

Add to this a different understanding that I had picked up from Mel Robbins at the same time. She compares passion to energy and describes it as something that comes from within rather than from something or someone external. It's that energy you feel inside yourself when you're doing something exhilarating or exciting.

This new combination of meaning was a paradigm shift around passion. There's all kinds of things that I've pushed through tough times for because they were exhilarating or exciting. Not only did it reframe the meaning of passion, but it also helped me realize that I can have more than one passion in any given moment and over my lifetime.

---

[9] passion. 2020. In Merriam-Webster.com. Retrieved November 14, 2020, from https://www.merriam-webster.com/dictionary/passion

As you evaluate these meanings of passion, take a moment to consider these questions:

What am I passionate about? Why?

What am I willing to go through the tough stuff for? Why?

What's so awesome that it gives me the perspective of "I don't care what it takes, I'm going to make it happen?" Why?

What am I willing to wake up at 3am on a Saturday, do for free, and never be able to add to my resume? Why?

Who am I when my heart is on fire?

What moves me to tears?

What injustice angers me the most?

What's missing right now as it relates to the passions I mentioned above?

What am I learning about myself as it relates to my passions?

What am I learning about who I am becoming through this activity?

Ideas for action:

Head Versus Heart

Today's Date: _____

At times, it can feel as if your head and your heart are at odds with one another. Your head tells you to be logical, while your heart yearns for something deeper. When you can get them on the same page, you can thrive in designing not only the life you want to live, but a life that is deeply integrated and fulfilling. Take a moment to consider these questions:

What does my head say about my future?

What is the internal dialogue I experience when I think about my future?

What does my heart say about my future?

What emotions do I experience when I consider my future?

If my head and my heart were to have a conversation, what would they say to one another?

How would each respond to what the other said?

What's the message my head has for my heart? Why?

What's the message my heart has for my head? Why?

How do they each need to compromise?

What am I learning about who I am becoming through this activity?

Ideas for action:

Facing Fear

Today's Date: _____

Several years ago, I came across an episode of the TED Radio Hour called Comfort Zone[10], which combined various TED Talks about how to get out of your comfort zone. One of the presenters, Tim Ferriss, shared a quote from Seneca that says, "we suffer more often in imagination than in reality." He went on to describe an activity that helps analyze and debunk fears that aren't well-founded.

 To hear this episode of the TED Radio Hour and Tim Ferriss's full TED Talk, scan the QR code here or visit www. lifelivedbydesign.com/facing-fear.

His TED Talk has been adapted here as a way to place your fears under a microscope to determine whether or not they are founded in any truth or accuracy. It might be helpful to reference the fears that were illuminated in the Resentment & Fear activity on page 112.

You will be returning to this activity in Part Four: Between. While it is not necessary to list twelve fears here, it will be helpful when you return to this later. With this said, complete this in a way that feels authentic and useful to you.

What are twelve things I would do if I had no fear and was guaranteed to succeed?

1.

2.

3.

4.

---

[10] Raz, Guy. (2018, April 27). *Comfort Zone.* NPR. https://www.npr.org/programs/ted-radio-hour/606073044/comfort-zone

5.

6.

7.

8.

9.

10.

11.

12.

For each of the fears above, complete the following chart and reflect on the additional questions. One chart is included here as an example, so you will need to leverage your journal or additional paper to fully complete this activity.

Fear #1 _____

What are all the worst-case outcomes of taking action on this fear?	What can I do to prevent that worst-case scenario?	How can I repair that worst-case scenario if it comes true?

What are all the worst-case outcomes of taking action on this fear?	What can I do to prevent that worst-case scenario?	How can I repair that worst-case scenario if it comes true?

What are all the benefits if I attempt or even experience partial success in taking action?

What's the cost of not taking action? If I do not take action on this, what will my life look like in a month, six months, a year, five years, twenty years?

Repeat this chart and reflection questions for each of your twelve fears.

What am I learning about who I am becoming through this activity?

Ideas for action:

TIP: This might be a great moment to revisit the Wheel of Emotions on page 26.

<u>Defining Your Fine Print</u>

Today's Date: _____

You've spent quite a bit of time in part three dreaming big, letting your imagination wonder, and unleashing your inner toddler who has no limitations. You might be feeling as though the results of the activities are redundant. That's an indication of one of two things: either you're not honoring your commitment to dig deep and spend time gut checking yourself or you're doing the work and are getting to the juicy stuff. Only you know the answer to that.

It is very intentional to have several similar activities back-to-back around envisioning your future. At some point in your youth a switch occurs. You go from being so confident that you will be President or land on Mars or become Wonder Woman or be in a band or, my personal favorite, be a turtle that eats bugs[11], but at some point in your journey you begin to receive messages from many different sources that tell you to be more realistic. You dream smaller, you lower the bar, and eventually you've forgotten altogether what you were once so confident about.

Just as important as it is to rediscover that side of you who doesn't place limitations on yourself, who dreams wildly, and who makes audacious claims, it is equally as important to get clear on what you don't want.

You know that pesky fine print. At some point, you've checked a box to acknowledge that you've read the user agreement or even signed the bottom of a contract indicating that you understand and agree to what is put forth. These agreements are crucial for the companies that put them out into the world because they protect the company and make sure they're not compromising or wavering on what they set out to achieve.

---

[11] HiHo Kids. (2017, July 6). *100 kids tell us what they want to be when they grow up.* YouTube. https://www.youtube.com/embed/RUup841pZrs?rel=0

In the same sense, you need to develop your own personal fine print - your user agreement or personal contract if you will. What are the things about which you absolutely will not compromise?

Let me give you an example. As you know, my true north is happiness. One of my non-negotiables is personal financial security. I also really love to travel. It makes me so happy to explore new places, meet new people, hear their stories, and push my perspectives and beliefs to new ways of thinking. With this said, I don't take every travel opportunity that is presented to me. If a trip compromises my personal financial security, I take a pass. It's a non-negotiable for me. See how that works?

This activity is designed to illuminate your non-negotiables. The aspects of life that you absolutely refuse, under any circumstances, to be a part of your journey.

Take a moment to consider these questions. Be specific.

When I consider the future I've fleshed out thus far (even if it's not quite crystal clear yet), what will be the biggest detractors in making it a reality?

What do I absolutely refuse to allow to be part of my life moving forward? Why?

What will I never do again, under any circumstances? Why?

What do I need to actively let go of? Why?

What aspects of the lives of those who are closest to me do I least resonate with? Why?

When revisiting the categories of my Wheel of Life, what about each category do I reject? For example, maybe as it relates to money, you refuse to have more than one credit card with a maximum limit of $2,500. Or, as it relates to friendships, you refuse to pour into friendships that no longer serve you. Or as it relates to career, you refuse to work for a company that does not align with your true north.

School:

Family:

Significant Other:

Health:

Travel:

Physical Space:

Fun:

Career:

Learning/Growth:

Spirituality:

Friendships:

Money/Finances:

Reflect, narrow down (if necessary), and compile my fine print here:

What am I learning about who I am becoming through this activity?

Ideas for action:

The Core

Today's Date: _____

In the "Determining Your True North" activity in part two, you spent some time clarifying what guides your present-day decisions. This is a critical barometer for assessing your most immediate decisions.

It is also important to gain clarity around what propels you forward. When you have a strong true north combined with an inner drive toward your future, there is nothing that can stop you. This simple activity is designed to help you dig to the core of what propels you into your future.

Based on the previous activities in part three, choose three aspects of your future vision that you want to begin taking action on. These don't have to be the most important or the most urgent. Instead, consider exploring the three that intrigue you the most or that you are most curious about. List them on the next few pages and follow the flow.

Intention #1

_____

Why is this important to me?

_____

And why is that important to me?

_____

And why is that important to me?

_____

And why is that important to me?

_____

What is at the core of this intention?

_____

Intention #2

_____

Why is this important to me?

_____

And why is that important to me?

_____

And why is that important to me?

_____

And why is that important to me?

_____

What is at the core of this intention?

_____

Intention #3

_____

Why is this important to me?

_____

And why is that important to me?

_____

And why is that important to me?

_____

And why is that important to me?

_____

What is at the core of this intention?

_____

Take a moment to consider these questions:

What am I noticing about what propels me into my future?

What themes do I notice among these three intentions?

What does the core of my intentions say about who I am being?

What does the core of my intentions say about who I am becoming?

How does the core of these intentions align or misalign with my true north?

What am I learning about who I am becoming through this activity?

Ideas for action:

TIP: You can come back to this simple process with any future intention to see how it aligns or misaligns with your true north.

In the End

Today's Date: _____

The renowned graffiti artist, Banksy, is quoted as saying, "They say you die twice. One time when you stop breathing and a second time, a bit later on, when someone says your name for the last time."

In the end, when all is said and done, your days have come to a close, and your name is only spoken in memory, what do you want your story to be? Not what you want your obituary to say or what you would want someone to share at a remembrance service, but the story YOU want told.

You have a story that you tell yourself, and it can either serve you or hold you back. For example, my story could be that I was born in the United States, and my parents divorced when I was just 6 years old. They both remarried and don't seem to be any happier in their new relationships. I struggled to make close friends growing up and felt a lack of connection to the community around me, so I took the first chance I had to leave. I moved across the country, where I felt even more isolated because I didn't know a single person before I moved there. I couldn't find a job in the city that I most wanted to live, so I felt stuck. I started doing all the "right" things to advance in my career, worked 50-60 hours a week, and had very little personal time. Then, out of nowhere, I was diagnosed with a brain tumor and my whole world turned upside down. I wasn't motivated in my career anymore and felt like I was floundering trying to find the next thing. Over the years, several people had told me I should be a coach, but I had brushed it off. When I found myself stumbling, though, I revisited the idea and decided that I'd start my own coaching practice. It has been an uphill battle to build my practice. Every single client I get takes a lot of work to enroll and some people who come to me and decide not to have me as their coach. Add to this the fact that I'm not only the coach doing the work, but I'm also the marketer, the accountant, the administrative assistant, the web developer, the writer, and the PR person. This is tough!

Or my story could be that I was born in the United States, where I had supportive parents and three amazing sisters who I adore. I have always had lots of friends that represent diverse perspectives of the world. This drew me to travel even more, so I could learn and grow through the others' experiences. It was a no brainer to move across the country when I got the chance. I always kept my eye out for the next professional opportunity that would challenge me and where I could contribute to making that institution better. I was thrilled when one of those opportunities happened to be in the city I love. I worked long weeks and loved the students I was serving. As I progressed in my career, I noticed that I was having less and less direct contact with students. So, I started to consider what else might be out there that would maintain the life I had built and give me more direct contact with students. Interestingly enough, about the same time, I was diagnosed with a brain tumor, and this skyrocketed my desire to not put off my life goals any longer. I came out of that experience stronger, happier, and with an even more crisp vision of what was ahead. I knew I needed to start my own coaching practice, and I love every minute of it, even the accounting and administrative work. Nothing is stopping me now, and I have no doubt every dream I have will come true.

I could have both of those stories, and, in fact, I do have both of those stories. Every single thing in both of those stories is true. But one of these stories serves me, and the other holds me back.

You are the only one writing your story. The book is on your desk. Yes, it's filled with pages of already written narrative, but there are even more blank pages to be filled. The exciting thing is that the pen is in your hand to start writing. You get to fill these pages however you want. You can start a new chapter, put in a plot twist, remove some unnecessary characters, or add new characters that contribute to the story you want to live. It's all in your hands.

Take a moment to consider these questions:

What story am I telling myself?

How does this story serve me?

How does this story hold me back?

What specific stories from my life (whether they've happened yet or not) do I hope people will share when I'm no longer here? Why?

What will these stories say about my character?

What will these stories say about what I valued?

What will these stories say about how I treated other people?

What will these stories say about how I treated myself?

What will make others laugh when they think about me?

What will make others cry when they think about me?

Who will tell my story? Why?

Utilize this space to write or draw about the story I want to tell that serves me.

What parts of this story have already come to fruition?

What parts of this story have yet to occur?

What do I need to learn to step more fully into this story?

What do I need to let go of to step more fully into this story?

Who do I need to be to step more fully into this story?

What am I learning about who I am becoming through this activity?

Ideas for action:

Ethical Will

Today's Date: _____

The idea of an Ethical Will is traced to Jewish tradition. It serves as a way to pass on ethical beliefs and values from one generation to the next. While there is a clear tendency and drive to focus on passing these beliefs and values to generations within your family, I encourage you to consider a communal ethical will. In other words, examine how you might pass on ideas, thoughts, values, perspectives, and beliefs to a whole community, country, or world.

Take a moment to consider these questions:

To whom do I want to address this ethical will?

Why is it important that the person or group of people I address hear what I have to say?

What is the core message I want them to know? Why?

What is the single most important idea I want to pass on? Why?

What's the legacy I hope to leave for others? Why?

What perspective will be most valuable to future generations? Why?

What values are most important to pass on? Why?

What beliefs are essential moving forward? Why?

Take a moment to craft these ideas and thoughts into an Ethical Will. Scan the QR code here or visit www.lifelivedbydesign.com/ethical-will to see examples.

Take a moment to consider a final point of reflection:

How can I more fully be a living example of my ethical will today?

What am I learning about who I am becoming through this activity?

Ideas for action:

TIP: This might be a great moment to revisit the Wheel of Emotions on page 26.

Personal Mantra

Today's Date: _____

I was in the midst of one of many road trips that I've taken throughout my life. This one took me throughout the New England area of the United States, and as I walked out of a Grist Mill, I found a stone bench to take a break. I noticed the front of the bench was engraved with the phrase "love the life you live."

I was immediately struck by it and found myself awkwardly lying on the gravel in front of the bench to get the perfect selfie position that would include both me and the quote. Not only did I want to remember it, but I wanted to know who said it.

When I arrived at my stopping point later that day, I found that the quote came from Bob Marley and that it was only a portion of his full thoughts. The entire quote reads:

Love the life you live. Live the life you love.

-Bob Marley

 To see this awkward photo, scan the QR code here or visit www.lifelivedbydesign.com/mantra.

This has since become my life mantra, and you may have noticed it in this workbook. Multiple times a day, I check in with myself to ensure that I am not only loving the current iteration of my life, but that I'm also intentionally creating a future life that I get excited about.

Mantras can be incredibly powerful. They serve as a grounding point, as a source of motivation and inspiration, and most importantly, as a personal (and sometimes professional) guide.

Craft your own personal mantra. Take a moment to consider these questions to help get your brain juices flowing:

What are my favorite quotes? Why?

What are my favorite songs? Which specific lyric from these songs stands out most? Why?

What would the title of this chapter in my life be if I were writing a book? Why?

What positive statements do I find I say to myself or others often? Why?

Write my personal mantra here.

How does my personal mantra embody my values?

How does my personal mantra connect with my true north?

How does my personal mantra take into consideration *where* I am now and *where* I want to go?

How does my personal mantra take into consideration *who* I am now and *who* I want to become?

What am I learning about who I am becoming through this activity?

Ideas for action:

TIP: Once you've landed on a personal mantra that speaks to you, post it in a place where you will see it regularly (on your bathroom mirror, on your closet door, on your steering wheel, or as a daily notification on your phone).

Toward Integration

Today's Date: _____

Now that you've explored your wild, crazy dreams and identified a few things you're passionate about, let's hone in on the overlap. This will set you up for action. The following diagram provides an opportunity to explore commonalities across passions, dreams, and intentions. Begin with each circle, which represents a different passion, intention, or dream, and work your way to the center as you continue to explore where these individual aspirations overlap into one. You may find it helpful to draw your own integration circles in your journal for more space.

Also, know that it's quite alright if you're not able to see where the overlaps are. This is an activity that might require more time and reflection than others to process. Take your time with this one. I began seeing the overlap in my circles while in college, but it took another 13 years to get to the core of it and see how they all integrated together into a cohesive lifestyle. Allow yourself the space and time needed for the integration to reveal itself to you.

To see my integration circles, scan the QR code here or visit www.lifelivedbydesign.com/integration.

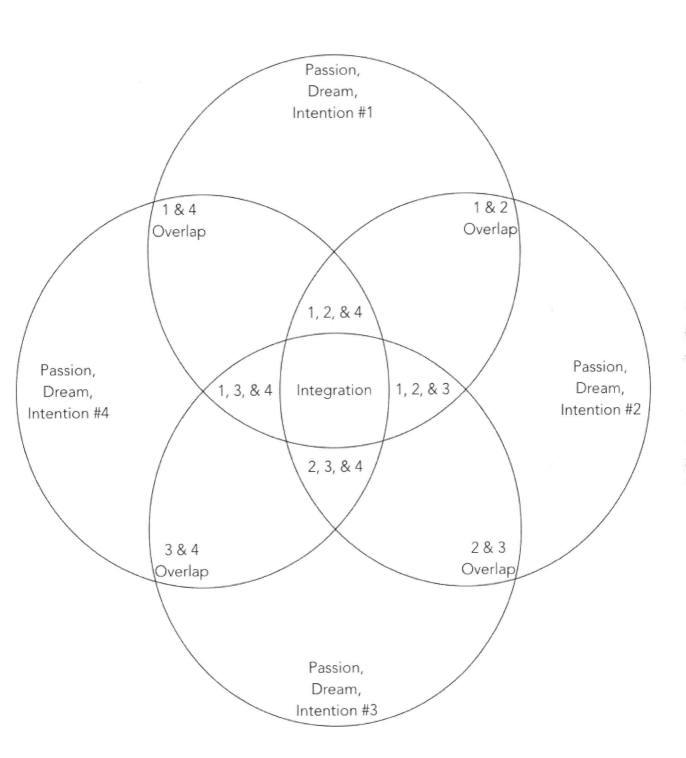

Take a moment to consider these questions:

What was easy about this activity? Why?

What was challenging about this activity? Why?

To what degree am I living an integrated life today?

What is holding me back from living a more integrated life?

Who do I need to be to step more fully into this integrated life?

Ideas for action:

Brain Dump

Today's Date: _____

Wow! What an incredible future you've defined for yourself! It's been an exciting journey that required you to tap into your imagination, let go of limitations, and examine what's possible. This work is exciting and energizing and, at the same time, it is hard to maintain long-term. You will experience roadblocks, obstacles, and doubtful people. When you remain focused on bringing your dream to reality, you will blow not only the minds of those around you, but also your own.

Before you move on to craft a plan of connecting your present to your future, do another brain dump. Pull out a timer and set it for five minutes. Press start, and use this space to free write for the entire time about what is present for you, having completed part three of this workbook.

Don't worry about spelling, grammar, incomplete sentences, legibility, or even whether you stay on topic or not. Simply write whatever comes to mind in whatever order it comes. You may even decide to draw instead of write words or a combination of art and words. Whatever you choose, let the pen flow, let your thoughts flow, and don't stop until the timer sounds.

No one will be reading this except you and those with whom you choose to share it, so let your thoughts flow freely. The purpose of this activity is to capture your future in totality as you see it from the position you're in now.

If you'd like a more pointed question, consider this: What am I most excited about for my future?

Ready. Set. Go!

TIP: Before starting part four, take a break (no more than a week, so you don't lose momentum). You are doing the work! Pat yourself on the back for remaining committed, and celebrate this milestone. Return to page 19 to remind yourself of how you planned to celebrate getting to this point.

TIP: This is also a great time to play the vision recording you created for yourself before starting this work.

TIP: This might be a great moment to revisit the Wheel of Emotions on page 26.

Part Four: Between

And the day came when the risk to remain tight in a bud was more painful than the risk it took to blossom.

-Anaïs Nin

Brain Dump

Today's Date: _____

Before you begin developing a plan for connecting your present to your future, take a moment to clear your brain of clutter. Pull out a timer and set it for five minutes. Press start and use this space to free write for the entire time. Don't worry about spelling, grammar, incomplete sentences, or legibility. Simply write whatever comes to mind in whatever order it comes. You may even decide to draw instead of write words or a combination of art and words. Whatever you choose, let the pen flow, and don't stop until the timer sounds.

No one will be reading this except you and those with whom you choose to share it, so let your thoughts flow freely. The purpose of this activity is to declutter your mind, so you can be fully present with the activities in part four.

Ready. Set. Go!

TIP: This might be a great moment to revisit the Wheel of Emotions on page 26.

Quick Wins

Today's Date: _____

As you transition into action, I want you to experience some quick, easy wins to jumpstart your plan moving forward. Take a moment to make a complete list for each column below:

All the things currently in my life that make me happy are:	All the things currently in my life that DO NOT make me happy are:

In the left column, circle three things that I can easily increase in my life. How specifically will I increase each of these things?

1.

2.

3.

In the right column, circle three things that I can easily decrease in my life. How specifically will I decrease each of these things?

1.

2.

3.

What will I start doing today?

What will I stop doing today?

What will I continue doing moving forward?

Motivation

Today's Date: _____

As you start taking action, take a moment to explore various ways of motivating yourself. Motivation falls into six general categories: intrinsic, extrinsic, proactive, reactive, for self, and for others. None is better or worse than the others. The key is to explore how each of these show up in your life and become more aware of how to strategically leverage each for your benefit.

Intrinsic motivation shows up when you commit to a project, task, or activity simply because you enjoy the process itself. The "doing" of the work is exciting and motivating. For example, writing a book simply because you enjoy the process of writing or eating dinner with your family every night simply because you enjoy the time together.

Where in my life am I motivated intrinsically?

How does intrinsic motivation contribute to my follow-through in certain areas of my life?

Extrinsic motivation shows up when you commit to a project, task, or activity because of the reward or outcome in the end. The results drive your action. For example, leveraging the reward of ordering your favorite dessert as an incentive to write part one of your book or pre-planning how you will celebrate the completion of this workbook.

Where in my life am I motivated extrinsically?

How does extrinsic motivation contribute to my follow-through in certain areas of my life?

Proactive motivation shows up when you commit to a project, task, or activity because it brings you closer to something you want. You progress toward something bigger. For example, writing a book that will also help you continue on your own posttraumatic growth journey or completing this workbook to know yourself better.

Where in my life am I proactively motivated?

How does proactive motivation contribute to my follow-through in certain areas of my life?

Reactive motivation shows up when you commit to a project, task, or activity because it pushes you away from something you don't want. You shift away from something that is not serving you. For example, sitting down to write for two hours because you don't want to tell your writing coach you didn't reach your intentions or developing healthier habits because you want to avoid diseases that might be in your family history.

Where in my life am I reactively motivated?

How does reactive motivation contribute to my follow-through in certain areas of my life?

Motivation for yourself shows up when you commit to a project, task, or activity because of how it impacts and benefits your own life. You see the value add in your life of following through. For example, writing a book to bust your own limiting beliefs about your abilities to do so or developing your spiritual life because of its impact on you.

Where in my life am I motivated for myself?

How does motivation for myself contribute to my follow-through in certain areas of my life?

Motivation for others shows up when you commit to a project, task, or activity because of how it impacts and benefits those around you, even those you haven't met yet. You see the value add in your community, your country, or the world. For example, writing a book because the world needs it or donating your time and money to help those in your community.

Where in my life am I motivated for others?

How does motivation for others contribute to my follow-through in certain areas of my life?

As you can see in the examples above, the same project can leverage multiple motivation techniques. The key is being able to identify when to leverage each type to your benefit. When I was struggling to write part one because its uniquely personal aspect, I decided to motivate myself with my favorite dessert. Once I got past part one though, I found that I was eager to sit down and write because I genuinely loved the process of seeing my ideas come to life. Later on in the writing process, I needed some coaching around my inner critic to remind myself why I was doing this in the first place. "The world needs this" became a hand-written note that I taped to my screen as a daily reminder.

As you progress through part four and begin to look at taking action, consistently ask yourself which motivation type you can leverage to follow through towards the outcomes you've designed for yourself.

TIP: Your vision recording can be leveraged for motivation as well.

TIP: When I am really in the pits, I pull out my hype list. It's a special playlist of songs that gets me going without fail every single time. Whether it's to kick me in gear on a project or simply to pull me out of a crummy mood, I can count on this hype list to get me where I need to go. What songs would you put on your hype list? Scan the QR code here or visit www.lifelivedbydesign.com/hype-list to check out the songs on mine.

Your Life Is Calling

Today's Date: _____

Your life calls you every single day. It's that tightness in your gut or that pull at your heartstrings or that inner voice in your head telling you there's more out there. You have an opportunity, every single day, to answer that call or send it to voicemail. You can engage in getting to know yourself on a deep level, crystallize the life you want to live, and make the rubber hit the road toward action. On the other hand, you can continue on a path that is not serving you, that is not fulfilling, and that does not excite you.

Your life is calling. To hear what it has to say, scan the QR code here or visit www.lifelivedbydesign.com/life-call. Before pressing play, find a comfortable space - one where you will not be interrupted, and you can allow your imagination to lead the way. As you listen, try not to be so worried about seeing a clear scene. What is important is the learning that comes from this activity.

Notes:

After taking the call from your life, take a moment to consider these questions:

What did my life have to say today?

What was surprising to hear? Why was that surprising?

What excited me about my life? Why is that exciting?

What or who do I need to confront in my life? Why?

What was the most challenging thing to hear from my life? Why?

What does my life love right now? Why?

What would my life like to change? Why?

What does my life want me to finish already? Why?

What does my life want from me more than anything else?

What was the core message my life had for me?

What would make the biggest difference in my life starting now?

TIP: This might be a great moment to revisit the Wheel of Emotions on page 26.

Leveraging Your True North

Today's Date: _____

It's estimated that adults make about 35,000 remotely conscious decisions every single day. From what to wear, to what to eat, to how we spend our time, we are making macro and micro decisions every moment of every day.

This means there are tens of thousands of opportunities to leverage your true north. Let's take a look at my true north of happiness as an example.

When I come to a place where I need to make a decision, I ask myself, "Will this immediately make me happy or keep me happy right now?" If the answer is yes, then I do it. If the answer is no, then I re-evaluate.

Notice I didn't say I don't do it. It's not that simple. As I re-valuate, I ask, "Will this get me closer to happiness down the road?" When the answer is yes, I do it. Sometimes, I have to do things in the moment that are unappealing, uncomfortable, or even impractical to get me closer to my true north.

However, if the answer to both of these questions is no, that's when I don't do it. If a decision is not currently in line with my true north AND it does not get me closer to achieving my true north in the future, I let it go.

As you begin leveraging your true north, I want you to start with big decisions. This might seem counter-intuitive, but it is the simplest way to integrate your true north into your daily life. Your biggest decisions are the ones that will have the most impact, and they're also the ones that generally have a clear alignment or misalignment with your true north. It's pretty easy to see whether big decisions will bring you to your true north or not. It also brings significant clarity to what could be a tough decision.

Consider the reverse of this approach. If you were to start by leveraging your true north in small decisions, you'd literally be battling with long-standing habits. Habits can be very difficult to interrupt. I want you to experience some quick wins with leveraging your true north so you're motivated to integrate it into all of your decisions, not just when it's convenient.

To leverage your true north, you're going to develop a question you can easily carry in your back pocket. One that you can pull out and ask yourself in the moment for any kind of decision-making. Will this make me happy right now? Will this make me money right now? Will this give me confidence right now? Will this give me freedom right now? Whatever your true north is, plug it in here.

When faced with a decision, I will ask myself, "Will this _____ right now?" This will allow me to align my actions with my intentions.

The second question to keep handy is, "Will it bring me closer to my true north?" Hold these together in your back pocket.

Put these in practice by completing the chart on the next page. A few things to note about this activity:
- Even if you know 100% that there is no way you would take action on a particular option in the first column, go ahead and list it anyway as practice.
- The second and third columns should be a simple yes or no response.

What is a decision I have coming up or one that I've been struggling to make?

What are all the possible actions I could take as I consider this decision?	Insert your first back-pocket question here: Will this option _____ right now?	Will this option bring me closer to my true north?

Take a moment to review your list and immediately cross off all the options with a "no" response in both the second and third columns. There's no reason you should be taking action in those ways.

Next, notice which options have "yes" responses in both the second and third columns. These are most likely going to be the most fulfilling options because they allow you to experience your true north now and in the future.

If you don't have any options that have a "yes" response for both the second and third column, that doesn't necessarily mean this decision isn't worth investing in. It's simply an indication that you may need to do some more reflection to determine the best option for you at this moment. This is where it becomes clear that just utilizing a compass and discovering your true north isn't enough. You also have to consider your fine print, which you identified in part three.

To help you get even closer to the best decision, refer back to your fine print on page 202. Cross off any options that are in contradiction to the fine print you crafted.

Take a moment to consider these questions:

My true north is _____ because it brings _____ into my life.

How will I leverage my true north in decision-making?

What does my true north say about who I am?

What does my true north say about who I am not?

What do I still want to learn about my true north?

How will I remember to leverage my true north?

10-10-10 Method

Today's Date: _____

When facing a tough decision (or a not so tough decision for that matter), I used to ask myself, "Will this matter in 100 years?" While this question gave me a ready-made perspective that took me beyond what I was immediately facing, it also removed intention from my decision-making. In 100 years, nothing was going to matter because I wouldn't be alive to know the difference.

Chip and Dan Heath, authors of the book *Decisive: How To Make Better Choices in Life and Work*,[12] share the 10-10-10 method, which I've found solves the issue of releasing intentionality, while still offering a ready-made perspective. They pose that you consider three time periods: 10 minutes, 10 months, and 10 years.

To illustrate this method, let's examine a decision you are currently facing. Write or draw about it here.

How do I imagine I will feel 10 minutes after having made the decision? Why?

---

[12] Heath, Chip & Heath, Dan. (2013). *Decisive: How to make better choices in life and work*. Currency

How do I imagine I will feel 10 months after having made this decision? Why?

How do I imagine I will feel 10 years after having made this decision? Why?

This method is powerful because in 10 minutes, you might feel angry, happy, excited, frustrated, etc. In ten months, depending on the size of the decision, you may or may not remember how you felt at all. Instead, you will most likely remember all the positive things from the situation. And, in ten years, unless it's a major life decision, you're probably not going to remember it at all.

This questioning allows you to step back from being so entrenched in the decision that you gain a totally different perspective. It helps you remove the emotions from the decision, so that you can make the best decision for yourself despite the emotions you're feeling.

TIP: As you progress into action, hold onto this 10-10-10 method as a way to check in with yourself on the balance between your head and your heart.

Vision to Promises to Action

Today's Date: _____

The path to your future is not the same as the path behind you. You can't expect to use the same techniques and strategies when you're leveling up as you did to get to where you are now. You have to do more. You have to do things differently. The process requires practice, learning from mistakes, multiple attempts, and different muscles and techniques. The practice you've had thus far has made you stronger for what's to come.

What is the vision you have for your life ahead? This includes aspects of your true north, your passions, your values, and your personal mantra. It's clear and, at the same time, less tangible, less measurable. For example, my life vision is to always strive for what brings happiness to me and those I love.

What is my vision?

From vision, you create your promises. This is where the tangible aspects come into play, and you begin to measure progress. What specific promises will bring your vision to reality? To continue with the example from above, a few of mine are:

- to visit every country in my lifetime
- to pay off my 30-year mortgage in 7 years
- to grow my coaching practice by 50% year over year
- to increase my personal income by 20% year over year
- to maintain my current weight
- to annually monitor my residual tumor for growth.

Each of these should be specific and include a number by which you can measure them.

What specific promises lead to my vision?

From promises, you take action. This is where the specific steps of bringing your promises to life come into play. To continue with one example from above, in order to visit all countries in my lifetime, parts of my plan includes:

- visiting roughly four countries each year
- setting aside at least $5,000 per country to visit without the worry of expenses
- establishing all coaching clients as virtual relationships

It may be helpful to revisit your "ideas for actions" in previous parts of this workbook. In doing so, make sure each of these actions leads to at least one of your promises and ultimately to your overall vision. If there is a misalignment, take time to consider how important it is to take that action or if you should let it go.

What are the specific actions that lead to my promises?

Take a moment to consider the following questions:

In order for me to implement this plan, to what must I say "no"?

If I say "no" to those things, to what am I, in turn, saying "yes"?

What action am I avoiding? Why?

How are this vision, promise, and plan aligned with my values from part two?

How are this vision, promise, and plan aligned with my true north from part two?

What character traits do I need to develop for this vision, promise, and plan to come to life?

The Zones

Today's Date: _____

You're well aware of your comfort zone, but did you know there are two other zones as well? Increasing your awareness of your adventure zone and your danger zone is just as important as awareness of your comfort zone.

First, make sure you have a clear understanding of each. Your comfort zone is exactly that - the zone in which you feel most comfortable. There is limited to no growth, and it is very safe. It's common to experience complacency in your comfort zone.

On the opposite end is the danger zone. In this zone, you experience legitimate fear, which can cause you to avoid action altogether. This zone is sometimes painful - physically, mentally, and/or emotionally. When you find yourself in the danger zone, you are typically in survival mode, trying to make it from day to day.

Between these two, you find the adventure zone. This zone is where you learn, grow, and evolve. It's exciting and scary at the same time. Unlike the danger zone, though, the scariness of the adventure zone does not manifest into legitimate fear and does not stop you from action. Also, unlike the comfort zone, you are not stagnant or complacent.

Below is a visual for each of these zones. Take a moment to place each of the actions from your plan on page 260 in one of the three zones. Ask yourself: Does taking this action keep me in my comfort zone, expand me into my adventure zone, or freeze me in my danger zone?

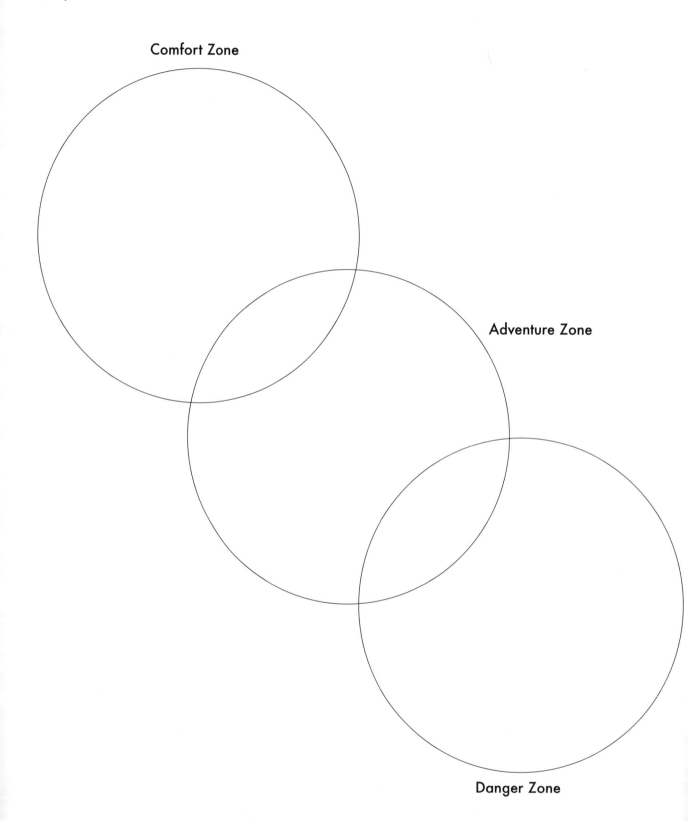

Comfort Zone

Adventure Zone

Danger Zone

Take a moment to consider these questions:

Which zone am I living in most often?

What is useful about being in this zone?

What is not useful about being in this zone?

What do I notice about the overlapping areas of my zones?

What am I not ready to change yet? Why?

What can I do in the meantime?

What adjustments do I need to make to my vision, promises, or actions in the previous activity?

Where to next?

TIP: This might be a great moment to revisit the Wheel of Emotions on page 26.

TIP: You can utilize these zones with any action list. We leveraged your action plan simply as a way to align the work you are doing.

Prioritizing Your Actions

Today's Date: _____

As you've progressed through this workbook, you've probably had a plethora of ideas for action. You may even have a full list in the notes section as you worked to release the urge to take action and sit in the increased awareness of yourself. In fact, you just created a plan for yourself that included specific action steps. Now it's time to make it happen - to connect the here with the there.

Figuring out where to start can feel overwhelming. This activity is designed to help you define and prioritize your ideas for action.

Begin by compiling all the ideas for action from throughout this workbook. Use this space or the notes section in the back of this workbook to bring them together and add any new ones. Consider those actions you need to take as well as those actions you want to take.

☐ _____   ☐ _____

☐ _____   ☐ _____

☐ _____   ☐ _____

☐ _____   ☐ _____

☐ _____   ☐ _____

☐ _____   ☐ _____

☐ _____   ☐ _____

☐ _____

☐ _____

☐ _____

☐ _____

☐ _____

☐ _____

☐ _____

☐ _____

☐ _____

☐ _____

☐ _____

☐ _____

☐ _____

☐ _____

☐ _____

☐ _____

☐ _____

☐ _____

☐ _____

☐ _____

☐ _____

☐ _____

☐ _____

☐ _____

☐ _____

☐ _____

☐ _____   ☐ _____

☐ _____   ☐ _____

☐ _____   ☐ _____

☐ _____   ☐ _____

☐ _____   ☐ _____

☐ _____   ☐ _____

☐ _____   ☐ _____

☐ _____   ☐ _____

☐ _____   ☐ _____

☐ _____   ☐ _____

☐ _____   ☐ _____

☐ _____   ☐ _____

☐ _____   ☐ _____

Once you have a complete list of actions, it's important to prioritize the list. This helps reduce the overwhelm and clear a path for moving forward. The charts on the next few pages are ways of prioritizing that I have leveraged at different points in my life. I recommend trying both to see which is most useful to you.

The first chart involves prioritizing based upon personal importance and urgency of the tasks. Several factors can contribute to the task's urgency, but the most common is a hard deadline. How important it is to complete a task is usually impacted by how that action aligns with your values. Each of your action items should fit into one of four quadrants:

- Quadrant 1 (Urgent and Important): These are items that are both important to you and need to be completed in the very near future to avoid any negative consequences.
- Quadrant 2 (Urgent and Not Important): These are items that may not be as important to you, but are an expectation from someone else. It could be beneficial to consider shoulder-tapping someone else to help with these tasks.
- Quadrant 3 (Not Urgent and Important): These are items that don't need to be completed in the near future and are still important to you. Typically, these tasks are related to long-term intentions.
- Quadrant 4 (Not Urgent and Not Important): These are things that usually serve as time-wasters (e.g., scrolling social media, cleaning to avoid other tasks, etc.). Ideally, you wouldn't intentionally plan action that falls into this category. However, it's helpful to be aware of it, so you can notice when you engage in these types of activities.

	Important	Not Important
Urgent	Quadrant 1	Quadrant 2
Not Urgent	Quadrant 3	Quadrant 4

In the next chart, you will prioritize the same action items by the impact created from completing them and how much effort it takes to complete them. Similar to the first chart, write each of your action items in one of four quadrants:

- Quadrant 1 (High Impact and Low Effort): These are your low hanging apples/quick wins. These are usually action items that can be completed relatively quickly, and you may have previously been avoiding them. You want to cross as many of these off without compromising your larger projects.

- Quadrant 2 (High Impact and High Effort): These are your big projects. They typically require more planning and preparation to complete and can often be broken down into smaller tasks to make them more bite-sized.

- Quadrant 3 (Low Impact and Low Effort): These action items tend to be your time-wasters, but not always. Check-in with yourself about each of these action items to ensure that these are necessary to take action on. If they are indeed necessary, leverage these tasks as a break from quadrant 2 or to keep your momentum going when you feel your energy declining.

- Quadrant 4 (Low Impact and High Effort): These action items usually require a lot of motivation to complete. If it's not necessary for you to do them, you might consider delegating them to someone else or looking for a way to collaborate with others to complete them. If you need to be the one to take these on, look for ways to bring fun to the task and give yourself a great reward when you finish.

	Low Effort	High Effort
High Impact	Quadrant 1	Quadrant 2
Low Impact	Quadrant 3	Quadrant 4

Regardless of which chart you leverage to prioritize your action items, the next step is to follow through on taking action. Pull out your calendar (either digital or paper) right now and schedule time for each of these action items. If there are any actions that you notice resistance to schedule, consider whether those actions are necessary or if they can be skipped altogether.

TIP: Take your schedule and self-accountability to an entirely new level with block scheduling. This is a well-known method of managing your time and your to-do list in a single format. A simple search for "block schedule" will provide a wealth of resources for assistance in this area.

TIP: Leverage these charts beyond this workbook's function by completing them each week to gain control over your to do list. At the end of the week, make note of how much you were able to accomplish in each quadrant, where you spent most of your time, and what adjustments you want to make for the coming week.

Build Your VIP List

Today's Date: _____

You know how there are certain things that you hear multiple times, but it doesn't really resonate with you until you hear it at just the right moment, in the just right way, and from just the right person? That was exactly my experience with this concept of building your success team. This was a concept I heard about for years before I was able to internalize it in a way that has had a lasting impact. It's changed the way I behave and interact with those most important to me.

It started out as a question. Who's in your corner? I brushed it off without giving it too much thought, saying, "Sure, I have friends and family who support me." This was my response for a long time.

About three years after I originally heard this, it was presented differently at a leadership development workshop. It went something like this: "You are a combination of the five people with whom you spend the most time." In other words, who are the five people who spend the most time in your corner? My response to this one was, "Well, I've moved around so much that I don't have anyone that I spend a lot of time with and, consequently, I don't know anyone that well. I've collected a lot of acquaintances over the years because I just can't sit still."

I was okay with that because I like being on the go. I still like being on the go and spending a little time with a lot of people rather than a lot of time with just a few people. While this version made me pause for a moment longer, I still brushed it off because I was so focused on the idea of spending time in person.

Fast forward another two years and I came across it yet again in a different way. The language was different, and I read it in a workbook rather than hearing it from a person. It went something like this: "Surround yourself with people who believe you can. List five people who can help you achieve your dreams and goals." Not only did I have to name specific people, but I also recognized that, in order for someone to help me achieve my dreams and intentions, I had to share the details out loud. That's when it hit me. This is more than having people in your corner or being intentional about how you give your time. This is about cultivating relationships that are reciprocal, trusting, and vulnerable.

I cried when I recognized that I could only write one name on that list, but this is where it impacted my behavior. After I wiped away the tears and I went into some deep reflection about who I wanted to have in my corner and who I wanted to have that type of reciprocal relationship with, I immediately went into action. I literally pulled out my phone and scrolled through the contact list to find those people. I added "VIP" to the end of their name. Now, I can search VIP in my contact list. I make a point to be very intentional about cultivating relationships with those people in a way that is both challenging and rewarding to both of us.

You might be thinking, *but how authentic is that relationship if you have to add VIP to hold yourself accountable?* I understand that perspective, but I also understood my weaknesses at the time. I knew that I was an "acquaintance-gatherer." The only way for me to break that habit was to intentionally set a new path for myself. I knew it would take time. I couldn't have snapped my fingers and made magic happen. I was prepared for the fact that some of the people who were on my VIP list when I started may not be there in a year or five years or 20 years for all kinds of reasons. I was also prepared to add to the VIP list as I continued to meet new people and reconnect with old friends.

In fact, all of that has happened since. Some folks have been removed from my VIP list, and others have been added. The list is fluid, as are relationships. The key is that I now have a way to be intentional, rather than leaving things to chance.

Those people who support you along your journey, lift you up, challenge you, push you towards continued growth, and with whom you can do the same serve as your VIP List. This activity allows you to identify your VIP List and what role each member plays in your corner. Being intentional about who you choose is crucial for establishing a support and challenge system to guide you along your journey.

List below those people who need to be on your VIP List, your relationship with each person, the role they play in your corner, the value each person adds to your life, and the value you add to their lives. The number of people on your VIP List is not as important as having enough people who provide guidance and diverse perspective. You also don't want so many that it becomes overwhelming. Think quality over quantity.

Name	Relationship to Me	Role in My Corner	Value They Add to My Life	Value I Add to Their Life

Name	Relationship to Me	Role in My Corner	Value They Add to My Life	Value I Add to Their Life

Take a moment to consider these questions:

What do I notice about my VIP list?

What do I most appreciate about my collective VIP list? Why?

What is missing from my VIP list? Why?

What do I have too much of in my VIP list? Why?

Who needs to be removed from my VIP list? Why?

Who needs to be added to my VIP list? Why?

How do I want to leverage my VIP list in accomplishing my vision and promises?

How am I showing up for those on my VIP list?

What support can I offer to those on my VIP list?

How will I continue to cultivate each of these relationships?

How will I express gratitude to those on my VIP list?

TIP: Open your phone and add "VIP" to the contact for each person on your list. Next, go to your calendar or reminders app and create a regular notification to remind yourself to cultivate each of these relationships proactively. Lastly, send a hand-written thank you note to each of your VIPs and drop it in the mail today.

TIP: On occasion, reach out to your VIP list for feedback. Some simple questions or conversations starts are

- How can I be a better friend/sibling/son/daughter/coworker?
- Why do you keep me in your life?
- Express gratitude for the relationship.
- What value do I add to your life?
- Share the value they add to your life.

Your Personal Resignation Letter

Today's Date: _____

You've spent a significant amount of time and effort crafting a vision, setting promises, and prioritizing actions for all the things you want to bring into your life. Equally as important is to take a moment to consider what you need to stop doing. Identify actions you're currently taking that are contrary to your vision, are not in alignment with your values, or are not bringing you closer to your true north.

When you write a resignation letter at work, you indicate to your employer that you will no longer be working at the company or organization. This resignation letter is to you. Indicate all the things you will no longer tolerate within yourself. Just as with a professional resignation letter, be sure to include the date on which you plan to resign, a brief explanation for why you are resigning, and an expression of gratitude. Be brief and direct with yourself. You may find it helpful to revisit the audit activities from part two as you complete this letter.

Dear _____,
        your name

I am writing to inform you that I am resigning from _____
                                                              activities you will stop doing

_____

_____

on _____. I have decided that _____
     date   reason for stopping said activities

_____

_____.

I am grateful for _____
                                expression of gratitude

_____

_____.

Sincerely,

_____
    your signature

TIP: Set a timeframe to regularly return to this letter as a quick, simple check-in on progress (e.g., the first of the month, every three months, every six months).

Overcoming Fear

Today's Date: _____

In part three, you created a list of twelve things you would do if you had no fear and were guaranteed to succeed. Twelve was a strategic number for that activity because there happen to be 12 months in a year. You've heard it before, the only way you overcome your fear is to face it. Over the next 12 months, you will be strategically facing each of these fears.

Now, this does not mean that you will experience 100% success, but it does mean you will experience extreme growth and learn incredible things about yourself. Utilize the space on the next few pages to craft your plan for each fear.

Month:

Fear #1:

What's the very first baby step?

Who's support do I need?

Which of my values will I exemplify by taking action on this?

Which perspective from page 150 will most serve you in overcoming this fear?

How does this get me closer to my true north?

What would my future self say about this?

What will overcoming this fear teach me about myself?

Month:

Fear #2:

What's the very first baby step?

Who's support do I need?

Which of my values will I exemplify by taking action on this?

Which perspective from page 150 will most serve you in overcoming this fear?

How does this get me closer to my true north?

What would my future self say about this?

What will overcoming this fear teach me about myself?

Month:

Fear #3:

What's the very first baby step?

Who's support do I need?

Which of my values will I exemplify by taking action on this?

Which perspective from page 150 will most serve you in overcoming this fear?

How does this get me closer to my true north?

What would my future self say about this?

What will overcoming this fear teach me about myself?

Month:

Fear #4:

What's the very first baby step?

Who's support do I need?

Which of my values will I exemplify by taking action on this?

Which perspective from page 150 will most serve you in overcoming this fear?

How does this get me closer to my true north?

What would my future self say about this?

What will overcoming this fear teach me about myself?

Month:

Fear #5:

What's the very first baby step?

Who's support do I need?

Which of my values will I exemplify by taking action on this?

Which perspective from page 150 will most serve you in overcoming this fear?

How does this get me closer to my true north?

What would my future self say about this?

What will overcoming this fear teach me about myself?

Month:

Fear #6:

What's the very first baby step?

Who's support do I need?

Which of my values will I exemplify by taking action on this?

Which perspective from page 150 will most serve you in overcoming this fear?

How does this get me closer to my true north?

What would my future self say about this?

What will overcoming this fear teach me about myself?

Month:

Fear #7:

What's the very first baby step?

Who's support do I need?

Which of my values will I exemplify by taking action on this?

Which perspective from page 150 will most serve you in overcoming this fear?

How does this get me closer to my true north?

What would my future self say about this?

What will overcoming this fear teach me about myself?

Month:

Fear #8:

What's the very first baby step?

Who's support do I need?

Which of my values will I exemplify by taking action on this?

Which perspective from page 150 will most serve you in overcoming this fear?

How does this get me closer to my true north?

What would my future self say about this?

What will overcoming this fear teach me about myself?

Month:

Fear #9:

What's the very first baby step?

Who's support do I need?

Which of my values will I exemplify by taking action on this?

Which perspective from page 150 will most serve you in overcoming this fear?

How does this get me closer to my true north?

What would my future self say about this?

What will overcoming this fear teach me about myself?

Month:

Fear #10:

What's the very first baby step?

Who's support do I need?

Which of my values will I exemplify by taking action on this?

Which perspective from page 150 will most serve you in overcoming this fear?

How does this get me closer to my true north?

What would my future self say about this?

What will overcoming this fear teach me about myself?

Month:

Fear #11:

What's the very first baby step?

Who's support do I need?

Which of my values will I exemplify by taking action on this?

Which perspective from page 150 will most serve you in overcoming this fear?

How does this get me closer to my true north?

What would my future self say about this?

What will overcoming this fear teach me about myself?

Month:

Fear #12:

What's the very first baby step?

Who's support do I need?

Which of my values will I exemplify by taking action on this?

Which perspective from page 150 will most serve you in overcoming this fear?

How does this get me closer to my true north?

What would my future self say about this?

What will overcoming this fear teach me about myself?

Eliminating Excuses

Today's Date: _____

As I consider the future vision for myself, what have I told myself (either during this examination or in the past) are all the reasons for why I can't or shouldn't have that future vision come to reality?

Instead, try this one on for size: _____ is not a priority for me right now.
future intention/vision

What happened when you named it as not a priority? Depending on the circumstance, you may feel a punch to the stomach or a sense of relief.

If you felt it was a relief, you need to go back and re-examine your reflections. You likely have not been totally honest with yourself about your dreams and vision of the future. There is likely still outside influence. You are probably still living for someone or something else, even if just in a small way.

For those who felt a punch to the stomach, it's time to stop kidding yourself. Stop telling yourself stories you know are not true. Stop holding yourself back. You are being your own worst enemy as it relates to living your designed life. It's time to set these excuses aside.

Who do I know (either personally or otherwise) who has accomplished a similar future vision to the one I imagine despite having setbacks, obstacles, or short-comings?

How can I leverage their story and experience as inspiration in moments of excuse, disbelief, or self-doubt?

TIP: If you feel you've done or tried everything and nothing is working, make a list of all the things you have tried. Literally, write them down on a sheet of paper. Now, consider what is not on that list. Saying that you've done or tried everything is a lie. It's an illusion. It's an excuse you tell yourself that prevents you from stepping into your designed life.

Simply Ask

Today's Date: _____

The answer to any question that goes unasked is always no. Always. 100% of the time, it is no. The result is that you find yourself in the same position that you're in right now. If this is the case, why would you ever not ask the question?

For example, asking for extra guacamole on your tacos. There's no guacamole on your tacos now, so the answer is already no if you don't ask. Asking for that promotion. You're not going to lose your job because you ask for a promotion and, if you don't bring it up, you're significantly reducing your chances of being considered.

Very, very rarely do you ask for something that ends up setting you back further than where you currently stand. You might even be pleasantly surprised by the response! The reality is that if you don't ask for what you're looking for, then the answer is most definitely going to be no by default, and your dreams will not come to fruition.

Take a moment to consider these questions:

What have I been afraid or nervous to ask for? Why?

What do I want in life more than anything else? Why?

What's holding me back from asking for it? Why?

What's the worst-case scenario if the answer is no?

What are the possibilities if the answer is yes?

What excuses do I need to let go of to make my ask?

What would happen if I did not make a "no" response personal?

What specifically am I going to ask for this week?

Don't Forget Yourself

Today's Date: _____

In this process of taking action, it may be tempting to slip into a routine of go, go, go, especially when the plan you've developed is something that excites you. You want to be careful, though, not to burn out along the way.

Just as you schedule time in your calendar to execute your actions, you also need to schedule time to refresh and revitalize yourself. Similar to creating a productive work space, you also need to create a sanctuary where you can disconnect and rejuvenate every aspect of yourself.

Take a moment to consider these questions:

When was the last time I did something big just for me?

What are the small things in my life that make me smile? Why do they make me smile?

What inexpensive or free things make me feel rich (not monetarily)? Why do they make me feel rich?

What do I need to revitalize myself and feel refreshed? Why?

What renews my excitement for life?

What tangible objects calm me down and relax me?

What activities release tension and stress?

What smells and sounds bring me to the present moment?

How do I show compassion toward myself?

TIP: Collect some of the objects, smells, sounds, and activities that bring peace to your life and create a small sanctuary in your home where you can easily take as little as one minute to regroup. Having a designated space that is always available creates an opportunity to leverage its power even in brief moments.

TIP: Identify three things you will commit to doing for yourself every single day. When things get tough, try not to let go of more than one of these three things.

TIP: Pull out your calendar and schedule time each day for these three things.

The Pillow Test

Today's Date: _____

When you put your head on the pillow at night, are you proud of who you were that day? Are you proud of what you accomplished? Are you proud of what you gave to those around you? Are you proud of what you gave to yourself?

If you lay your head down at night and your answer is "no" to any of these, there are two things you can do:

    (1) Ask yourself, "What can I do in the next five minutes to turn this around?"

    (2) Think toward tomorrow. "What can I do tomorrow to ensure I pass my pillow test tomorrow night?"

Notice that neither of these includes getting down on yourself or letting your inner critic tell you you're not good enough. The point is to reflect and learn so that you do better tomorrow.

Let's start today:

Am I proud of who I was today?	Yes	No
Am I proud of what I accomplished?	Yes	No
Am I proud of what I gave to those around me?	Yes	No
Am I proud of what I gave to myself?	Yes	No
Am I proud of how I aligned with my true north today?	Yes	No

For those to which I answered "no," what can I do in the next five minutes to turn this around?

For those to which I answered "no," what can I do tomorrow to ensure I mark "yes?"

TIP: This may be a moment where your inner critic pops up to put in their two cents. Flip back to page 124 to remind yourself of how you planned to handle this little character when it pops up.

TIP: This might be a great moment to revisit the Wheel of Emotions on page 26.

Building Resilience

Today's Date: _____

No plan is executed flawlessly, seamlessly, or without hurdles or setbacks. Resilience is the key to overcoming and pushing past obstacles in a way that makes us stronger on the other side.

The word resilience comes from the Latin root 'resilire' meaning "to jump back or recoil."[13] Developing resilience is literally the process of choosing to bounce back in the face of defeat. When we take this a step further through the lens of posttraumatic growth, it's leveraging setback as an opportunity to bounce forward, beyond where you were before.

To build resilience, it is important to consider seven key areas:

1. Clarity of the outcome
2. Clarity of potential obstacles
3. Resources & community
4. Agency
5. Willingness to take ownership
6. Openness to feedback
7. Ability to express gratitude

As you progress through this activity, consider the person you want to become (possibly your future self from part three) in each of your responses.

---

[13] resilient. 2020. In Merriam-Webster.com. Retrieved November 14, 2020, from https://www.merriam-webster.com/dictionary/resilient

Clarity of the outcome: How clear to you is the person you want to become?

Clarity of the outcome: How clear is the larger impact of becoming this version of yourself?

Clarity of potential obstacles: What might get in your way of becoming this person?

Clarity of potential obstacles: How can you proactively plan for overcoming obstacles?

Resources & community: What resources - both tangible and intangible - are at your disposal to help you become that person (material, time, energy, financial, people, etc.)?

Agency: To what degree do you believe in your own ability to become this person?

Willingness to take ownership: To what degree are you willing to take ownership of the process toward becoming this person?

Openness to feedback: To what degree are you open to receiving feedback in the process of becoming this version of yourself?

Ability to express gratitude: How will you express gratitude along your journey?

TIP: Any responses that evoke dissatisfaction within you indicate areas for continued growth and exploration. Working with a coach is very helpful for this type of work.

Developing Agency

Today's Date: _____

As you explored in part two, agency is your belief in your own abilities. A hugely important aspect of developing your personal agency is collecting evidence that verifies your belief in the possibilities. You have plenty of evidence from your past to show you are capable of living an exceptional life. You simply fail to bring it forward at times because you might be focused on what went wrong.

Today, you are going to start your evidence log. This is the evidence that will ultimately develop your agency - your self-belief. List below all the evidence that you personally have in your life that makes the following statement true.

I can live an exceptional life - one that is examined and fulfilled.

TIP: This page is intentionally left blank. Tear it out and post it somewhere prominently in your home or at work. Refer to it when you need a reminder that you, too, are capable of designing a life worth living. As you accrue new evidence moving forward, continuously add to this list.

TIP: You can create an evidence log for any area of your life where you'd like to develop agency. Simply adjust the initial statement by filling in the blank: Maybe I can…

Revisiting the Wheel of Life

Today's Date: _____

You started this workbook with the Wheel of Life as a great snapshot of where you began in different aspects of your life. It's time to revisit this activity to explore the growth you've experienced along this journey.

1. Start by adjusting any of the categories you see around the circle. Maybe you want to remove, rename, or add new categories. Maybe you want to split a category into subcategories. Go ahead and make the wheel your own. You might also find that the wheel, as it currently exists, suits you well. It's also okay to leave the categories as they are.

2. Consider your level of satisfaction in each wedge independently and give it a score of 1-10 where 1 is, "I'm really not satisfied with this area of my life," and 10 is, "I'm super satisfied with this are of my life." It's important to consider your current level of satisfaction today, not where you'd like it to be. Write your rating next to each category on your wheel.

3. For the last step, go ahead and shade in the wheel to represent the number you gave each wedge.

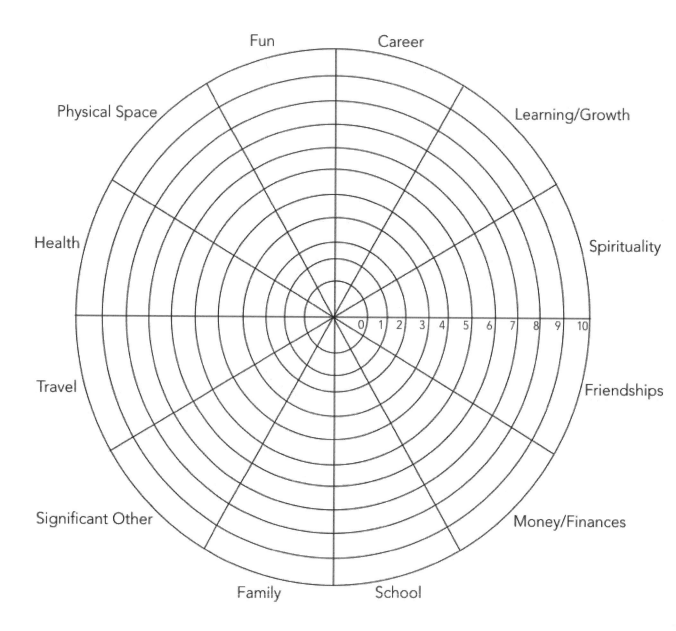

Take a moment to consider these questions:

Other than the numbers themselves, what jumps out at me about my wheel? Why?

In looking back at my original Wheel of Life, what changes do I notice?

What happens when I place myself at the center of the wheel?

What character traits have I strengthened in this journey?

What did it take to get to where I am now?

What am I most proud of during this journey?

Who do I have to become to make my dreams a reality?

What am I most excited about who I am becoming?

Non-traumatic Growth Inventory

Today's Date: _____

As was mentioned in part one of this workbook, the goal is to provide you with a level of posttraumatic growth without experiencing trauma. To this end, this inventory has been created as a means to assess your journey. It is important to note that this inventory is not empirically validated and is meant to serve as a capstone to this workbook.

Consider each of the statements below according to this scale:

0 - I **did not** experience this as a result of completing this workbook.

1 - I experienced this to a **small degree** as a result of completing this workbook.

2 - I experienced this to a **moderate degree** as a result of completing this workbook.

3 - I experienced this to a **significant degree** as a result of completing this workbook.

4 - I experienced this to a **substantial degree** as a result of completing this workbook.

_____ I have a clearer understanding of all aspects of my life.

_____ I have increased the investment in myself.

_____ I have a stronger sense of my values.

_____ I make decisions based in these values.

_____ My truth is derived from my own opinions and beliefs, rather than from others.

_____ I have a clearer understanding of how to leverage resources to my benefit.

_____ I have relationships that are mutually beneficial.

_____ I am managing my inner critic.

_____ I have a better understanding of how I show up in the world.

_____ I have a greater sense of self.

_____ I notice when my thoughts are not serving me.

_____ I have a clearer vision of my future.

_____ I know who I am working to become.

_____ I know the impact I could have on the world.

_____ I understand what drives me forward.

_____ I am confident in overcoming obstacles along my journey.

_____ I live a more integrated life.

_____ I take ownership over the results in my life.

_____ I believe I have what it takes to bring my dreams to reality.

_____ I am committed to getting closer to my true north every day.

_____ It is clear to me what is really important in life.

_____ I have a renewed zest for life.

_____ I am willing to embrace all emotions.

_____ I can easily express gratitude.

_____ I have a greater sense of interdependence.

Total = _____/100

Take a moment to consider these questions:

What do I notice about my growth?

Where do I go from here?

Brain Dump

Today's Date: _____

Congratulations! You made a statement to yourself when you chose this workbook and a commitment when you picked up the pen to begin the work. You've examined every aspect of your life with a magnifying glass to pick it apart and rebuild it into a life you are excited to live. This bold journey has required significant vulnerability to arrive at this point, and that's exactly where you are - a point, not a destination.

You have not arrived. You have not completed the work. What you have done is discovered who you are today, who you want to become, and how to connect those two. In essence, you have learned how to experience a life lived by design. You have everything within you to navigate your life in a way that serves you, and THAT is powerful. You are equipped to make any life you want a reality for yourself.

When you feel yourself getting off track or distracted, come back to this workbook. Start from the beginning and follow it through until the end or leverage those tools and activities that you most need at that moment.

Before you move forward, let's do one final brain dump. Pull out a timer and set it for five minutes. Press start, and use this space to free write for the entire time about what is present for you having completed the entire workbook.

Don't worry about spelling, grammar, incomplete sentences, legibility, or even whether you stay on topic or not. Simply write whatever comes to mind in whatever order it comes. You may even decide to draw instead of write words or a combination of art and words. Whatever you choose, let the pen flow, let your thoughts flow, and don't stop until the timer sounds.

No one will be reading this except you and those with whom you choose to share it, so let your thoughts pour out freely. The purpose of this activity is to capture where you are in this moment, who you are in this moment, and who you are becoming.

Ready. Set. Go!

TIP: Play back your vision recording to see what was manifested, what was adjusted, and what you let go of.

TIP: This might be a great moment to revisit the Wheel of Emotions on page 26.

A Final Step

Today's Date: _____

As is alluded to in this workbook's title and described in part one, this work is life-long. It does not end here. In fact, it does not end anywhere. This is just the beginning and that should be exciting! You never truly arrive. Yet, there is an opportunity to arrive each day.

Revisit the intentions you set on page 22 and take a moment to consider these questions:

How have my intentions come to fruition?

What would I like to acknowledge about who I have been throughout this journey?

How is my life different after doing this work?

What commitment do I want to make to myself moving forward? Why?

Each August, I make my way to the hospital for an MRI and an appointment with my neurosurgeon to monitor the residual tumor. The intention is to catch any growth early enough that a treatment plan can be implemented to reduce the impact of that growth. This check-in parallels my own personal check-in on the commitments I made to myself shortly after my surgery. Am I loving the life I live? Am I living the life I love?

Revisiting your commitments to double down, adjust, or release them is a critical part of this bold journey. It ensures that you are always living an examined life. Today, make a commitment to yourself to make this a life-long process.

I will revisit this workbook to assess my progress, make adjustments, and continue living an

examined life. I will start that recommitment process on _____.
                                                                           date

_____
      signature

Now, go to that date in your calendar to set a reminder for yourself to follow through on this commitment.

Most importantly, it's time to celebrate! Go back to your plan on page 19 and get your celebration on because you've just stepped into living an examined life!

<u>Final Thoughts</u>

It's commonly known that bamboo grows very quickly. It breaks ground at its full diameter and grows to its full height in a single season. Some species can grow 36 inches in just one day!

But there is something about bamboo that is spoken of less. It takes several years for it to break ground. Years! Not days, weeks, or months - YEARS! It's working underground to establish itself, to prepare for the magnitude of what the root system holds and, essentially, to get it right.

Sometimes when you are working toward an incredible future, you can lose sight of what all the work is for. Many of the best and biggest accomplishments you will experience in your life don't come overnight. You establish yourself, prepare for what's to come, and work to get all the pieces in the right place, so that when everything comes together, your hard work pays off in magnitudes.

As I shared in the "Defining Fine Print" activity, one of my non-negotiable is marriage. I do not have any desire to be married, which means my left ring finger has been empty while those around me have all made that commitment to someone else. In late 2017, I decided I was ready for that level of commitment. I went to a local jeweler, chose a beautiful ring with a blue topaz surrounded by

diamonds, and committed to myself that I would never go back to the life I lived before my diagnosis. To see a photo of this commitment, scan the QR code here or visit www.lifelivedbydesign.com/ring.

You don't need to go out and spend money on something extravagant to remind yourself of the commitment you are making. Here are some other ways you can remind yourself of this work:
- Messages on your bathroom mirror
- Alerts that pop up on your phone when you need them most
- Notes on the steering wheel of your car
- Screensavers on your phone and laptop
- Vision recordings that you can play no matter where you are

- Reminders on your door as you walk out of your home
- Song associations

My challenge to you is to commit yourself to continue your bold journey. Continue it now, continue it when the payoff comes, and most importantly, continue it when the payoff has worn off. Remember that it didn't come overnight and probably didn't come easily all the time. Hold onto these lessons.

Results for Compass Versus GPS

When I consider an intention…

(compass)   I am able to see multiple paths to accomplishing that intention.

(GPS)   I can see exactly what I need to do to bring it to reality.

When I come upon obstacles…

(compass)   I feel challenged and take a moment to consider all of my options.

(GPS)   I feel overwhelmed and take a moment for a break.

When I listen to my internal dialogue…

(compass)   I am flexible in considering the best way forward.

(GPS)   I am determined to make things work, no matter what.

When I receive feedback…

(compass)   I consider the information to make better decisions.

(GPS)   I am confused about how to apply it to my current circumstances.

<u>Notes</u>

<u>Notes</u>

Notes

<u>Notes</u>

<u>Notes</u>

With Deep Gratitude

Thank you to Dr. Matthew Tate and the incredible team both at Northwestern Memorial Hospital and at Northwestern Medicine Lou and Jean Malnati Brain Tumor Institute for the exceptional care and genuine compassion you have shown me since January 5, 2017.

Thank you, Alicia Samuels-Whitman, Antoinette Cummings, Bryana Ware, Jenny Minsberg, and Rachel Adams, for so generously sharing your time, energy, effort, and brainpower as reviewers of the first draft of this workbook. Your insights and contribution to this project are immeasurable.

Thank you, Brittney Leigh, for your amazing support as my Writing Coach throughout this process. I would not have gotten to publication without your guidance and support.

Thank you to every single person who has provided a five-star review on Amazon to help others experience non-traumatic growth.

Thank you, family, for embracing and supporting my unique purpose.

Thank you, brain tumor, for waking me up and prompting me to live an examined life - one that is by design.

Thank you, ME, for leveraging this trauma as a growth opportunity and creating the space that moves me toward knowing myself.

Author Bio

Brittany Salsman (she/her), a former educator, was checking all the boxes until everything abruptly changed in 2017. A diagnosis of a brain tumor launched her into a life-long relationship with posttraumatic growth. She now leverages this experience as an International Coach Federation (ICF) credentialed life coach to help others experience transformational growth without the necessity of a life-altering event - what she calls non-traumatic growth. She fundamentally believes that everyone wants to be known and that starts with knowing yourself first. Her clients explore where they are now, who they want to become, and how to connect the two. They walk away with a deeper, more intimate knowing of themselves that allows them to experience a Life Lived by Design.

In addition, she has the honor of being part of others' journeys toward becoming a certified life coach by serving as a Coach Trainer with Coach Training EDU.

In her free time, Brittany travels in her converted van with her Yorkipoo, Taz. She has promised herself she will visit every country in her lifetime and wants to collect more stories than she has time to share them. She is committed to loving the life she lives and living the life she loves every day.